Railway
Roundabout

Railway Roundabout

A Guide to the Highlights of the TV Series

Rex Christiansen

IAN ALLAN
Publishing

First published 1997

ISBN 0 7110 2456 1

© Ian Allan Ltd 1997

Published by Ian Allan Publishing

an imprint of Ian Allan Ltd, Terminal House, Station Approach, Shepperton, Surrey TW17 8AS. Printed by Ian Allan Printing Ltd, Coombelands House, Coombelands Lane, Addlestone, Surrey KT15 1HY.

Half title page: A dramatic view of the incline at Cromford on 18 May 1966 shows the gradient facing locomotive crews as they battled over this route. *R. C. Riley*

Title page: Two of the features of its series were the recording of locomotive classes that were about to disappear and the preserved locomotives that were to appear in the late 1950s. Here, at Star Lane on 15 September 1963, the ex-Caledonian Single No 123 and the ex-London & South Western 'T9' No 120 are caught double-heading a special to Haywards Heath and the Bluebell Railway (itself featured in one of the programmes). No 123 featured in the series as part of a record of the preserved Scottish Region locomotives and the 'T9s' appeared in a programme depicting their operations in the West Country. *R. C. Riley*

Below: Pictured in September 1953, No 7 is seen in plain black livery still retaining 'GWR' on the side of the tanks and with a painted number on the buffer beam, rather than the cast number plate that was to be affixed shortly afterwards. The locomotive was photographed departing from Aberffrwd with a rake of coaches in the carmine and cream livery. *T. B. Owen/Colour-Rail (BRW1295)*

Contents

Foreword

It all seems a very long while ago that we started *Railway Roundabout*. It came about quite by chance after Pat Whitehouse and I met over the Talyllyn Railway and, as a result, we made one or two films together, which we showed to our family and friends. One day my wife and I were round at a neighbour's house and he said that his sons had told him that I had some films on railways. This neighbour was Dennis Morris, who was head of BBC Programmes for the Midlands. 'Just the thing for your children's program-mes,' I said. The outcome was an invitation to meet the Head of Children's Programmes in the Midlands, Peggy Bacon, with Pat Whitehouse.

The programme contract was with John Adams and we bought all the film, as I was a professional photographer. The BBC paid Pat and myself, and we then split any profits that we made, which were not much! Once we were established, we had free passes on BR which were a great help.

In the end we had to appear live in the programme, which was broadcast in the years before tele-recording. It was also broadcast in black and white.

Some of the films were made about 18 months before broadcast, as we had to keep a stock of material. Our first films were made entirely on spec — they were Isle of Man, County Donegal, Cavan & Leitrim, Abergavenny & Merthyr and an Ian Allan special to Swindon. In all we made 100 films and there were 52 programmes. There were no programmes during July and August and most of the filming was done during this period. Rex Chrstiansen has done a good job with his research.

John Adams, FRSA, ARPS
November 1996

Right:
John Adams pictured whilst filming the 'Caley Bogies from Perth to Aviemore' at Perth. *Courtesy of John Adams*

List of Locations

Introduction

The *Railway Roundabout* programmes were made during one of the most historically interesting periods in the history of British Railways. The programmes began three years after the BR Modernisation Plan of 1955 was announced and they ended the year before the Beeching Report. The biggest changes which interested enthusiasts were probably those of motive power as steam gave way to diesel and, in some areas, electric traction.

The programmes have developed far beyond their original concept of being made for the enjoyment of young viewers and are now of national historic importance. Yet such heavy thoughts need not bother an enthusiast who just wants to enjoy a little nostalgia, for they are full of that.

There is emphasis on steam and on lines that had closed or were threatened with extinction, but there is no attempt to present an overall picture of any particular aspects of railways. My regret is that the series stopped in 1962 and that whatever footage was unwanted at the time was swept from the film cutting-room floor and thrown away. This is also a regret I feel about many of the railway programmes broadcast on BBC national and regional television and radio with which I was associated.

The videos are a reminder of a world from which much has vanished — and much has been saved and enhanced for future generations. I think especially of the preserved railways that the *Railway Roundabout* team visited at a crucial time in their history when they were being developed as all-the-year-round family and tourist attractions.

Railway Roundabout has been written to supplement the videos so the text does not generally include details given in the commentaries by Peter Woods.

Bibliography

Books that I found exceptionally informative are noted at the end of each section. Information about lines, locomotives and operating methods shown in the videos are to be found in numerous books, including *The Regional History of Railways* and *Forgotten Railways* series, originally published by David & Charles, and in individual company histories.

Railway magazines, especially issues published between 1958–62, annual editions of *Railways Restored* and *Branch Line Index*, a guide to major articles in several magazines, published by the Branch Line Society, were other useful sources.

Below: The Eastern Region was not covered significantly in the series, but one episode did recall the final 2-4-0 in passenger service at Cambridge. This is a general view of Cambridge and shows, on the left, Class D16 4-4-0 No 62543 and, on the right, Class B17 4-6-0 No 61600 *Sandringham* on 16 May 1957. R. C. Riley

'Terrier' No 32678, originally LBSCR No 78 *Knowle*, is pictured at the junction station of Havant awaiting departure with a service for Hayling Island on 8 September 1962. *R. C. Riley*

1958

Abergavenny & Merthyr

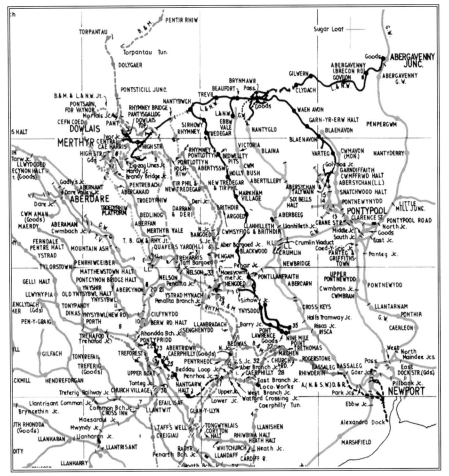

The *Railway Roundabout* programmes began with a spectacular farewell to passenger services over the most spectacular railway in South Wales.

The last passenger train between Abergavenny and Merthyr over the Heads of the Valley route was a Stephenson Locomotive Society special which West Midlands Area members ran on Sunday 5 January 1958.

The film was shown in the first edition of *Railway Roundabout* transmitted on BBC1 on 20 April when memories were still fresh in the minds of hundreds of its passengers.

The Beeching Report which was to destroy some main lines and many secondary and branch lines, still lay five years in the future. But the Abergavenny & Merthyr economy is remembered as a prime example of the pruning of passenger services begun in the late 1940s, soon after the end of World War 2.

It might have seemed hardly auspicious to launch a major TV series by featuring the withdrawal of a 25-mile passenger service, but the irony passed without comment.

That was perhaps because John Adams and Pat Whitehouse captured a journey memorable for reflecting the atmosphere of deep sadness and nostalgia surrounding closures that was to reach its peak in the Beeching era.

Two Crewe-built Webb locomotives double-headed the special and blasted smoke high into the sky as they struggled to master gradients stiffening to 1 in 34 on a climb of seven miles which lifted the line to 1,200ft above sea level.

The train engine was 'Super D' 0-8-0 No 49121, of which a number were still in service, but it was the pilot which caught the enthusiasts' attention for it was the last of Webb's much admired coal tanks: No 58926. Soon afterwards it was bought and preserved by J. M. Dunn who recalled his work among such engines in South Wales and elsewhere in his autobiography *Reflections on a Railway Career* (Ian Allan 1966).

Both locomotives represented sturdy classes with which the LNWR, and later the LMS, brought their own distinctive presence to South Wales as they competed for traffic against the GWR, which dominated the coalfield.

The special also commemorated economies affecting several short branches which stemmed from the Heads of the Valley line. There was a farewell run down the one-and-a-half miles from Beaufort to Ebbw Vale (High Level), and a bank-back to the main line because the engine could not run round.

The branch had lost its local passenger service to Brynmawr seven years earlier, but had remained open for freight. This was to cease in November 1959.

Several miles closer to Merthyr, Rhymney Bridge was the junction for an equally short branch to Rhymney, developed jointly by the LNWR and the Rhymney Railway. Although the Western Region had withdrawn the third-class only local passenger service and closed the branch in September 1953, SLS members rekindled memories by naming it on one of two buffer-beam boards carried by the locomotives. It was also included in the title of the black-edged souvenir programme.

Reading
Tasker, W. W., *The Merthyr, Tredegar & Abergavenny Railway and Branches*

Abergavenny (Brecon Junction)– Merthyr (Rhydycar Junction)
Distance: 24 miles
Owner: London & North Western Railway
Opened: From 1862. LNWR trains ran to Merthyr from 1879
Closed: 22 November 1954 Abergavenny–Merthyr for Through Goods
6 January 1958 Abergavenny–Merthyr for Passengers

Beaufort (Ebbw Vale Junction)–Ebbw Vale High Level
Distance: 1¼ miles
Owner: London & North Western Railway
Opened: 1867
Closed: 1 February 1951 for Passengers
2 November 1959 for Goods

The Cardigan Branch

The commentator of the series was Peter Woods, for years a well-known national television newsreader. He pointed out that the Cardigan branch was the antithesis of the 'Bristolian' which it followed.

The single line of the branch left the South Wales main line at Whitland, 234 miles from Paddington and 27 miles east of Fishguard. It meandered 27½ miles to Cardigan, a classic GWR single-platform branch-line terminus. Even though only a small station, it had a staff which included a station master, porters, booking-office staff, signalmen and shunters.

Closure, blamed on road competition, was spread over several years. Passenger services ended in September 1962, ahead of the Beeching Report, and ordinary goods services were withdrawn the following May after Beeching, although coal traffic continued until 1965.

The September 1958 Western Region passenger timetable No 150 headed Whitland, Crymmych Arms and Cardigan, showed four down services to Cardigan and three up from the busy market town. They took about 1hr 40min, making calls at five stations and four halts. The timetables showed Cardigan as the station for Gwbert-on-Sea, a seaside village 3¼ miles away.

The Cardigan branch ran through quiet, thinly-populated countryside. An Edwardian guidebook writer described the journey as 'picturesque almost throughout', but that was perhaps not the way engine crews saw it for there were stiff gradients on a number of stretches, the worst at 1 in 60.

The one-coach, second class only, weekday only trains were sometimes mixed, a covered van being marshalled between the coach and the locomotives. Two ex-GWR types were working the branch when it was filmed: small '45xx' 2-6-2 prairie tanks and small Hawksworth '16xx' 0-6-0 pannier tanks. These were the GWR's last design of light-passenger tank engines.

No 4450 was handling the passenger working and No 4558 dealt with the still quite heavy goods traffic. The panniers also headed the passenger workings.

The village of Crymmych Arms (the branch terminus from 1875 until it was extended to Cardigan in 1886) sometimes echoed to the staccato bark of both types of locomotives as they headed away in opposite directions from the passing loop.

Reading

Clark, R. H., *An Historical Survey of Selected Great Western Stations: Layouts and Illustrations, Volume 1*

Burrell, J. F., *The Railway Magazine*, July 1952

Cardigan Junction–Cardigan	
Distance:	25 miles
Owner:	Great Western Railway
Opened:	1873–1886
Closed:	10 September 1962 for Passengers
	27 May 1963 for Goods

Below:
'16xx' 0-6-0PT No 1666 arrives at Cardigan in August 1962 with the 11.35am service from Whitland. The 70 members of this class were constructed post-Nationalisation to a design produced by Hawksworth, the last CME of the Great Western Railway. *P. W. Gray/Colour-Rail (BRW237)*

Right:
Looking slightly careworn in the summer sun, '45xx' class 2-6-2T No 5520 awaits its next duty at Cardigan alongside the River Teifi in June 1962. *Colour-Rail (BRW1270)*

Below:
Equally careworn, sister locomotive No 5550 is pictured at Login on 26 March 1962. The period detail of level crossing, crossing box and platform staff bring the railways of that era to life — not to mention the elderly lady carefully crossing the line in the foreground. *Colour-Rail*

The 'Bristolian'

Filming the 'Bristolian' in 1958 was fortuitous for it was the last year it was a famous steam-hauled titled train. The name was dropped in 1959 when 'Warship' diesel-hydraulic locomotives took over from 'Castle' and 'King' locomotives. Later they were displaced by 'Bristol Pullman' diesel electric sets. They ran until London–Bristol services assumed their present form of unnamed HST expresses in September 1976 and began, with those between Paddington and South Wales, the fastest diesel rail service in the world.

The HSTs consigned to history many achievements of the 'Bristolian' which in 1958, was the only British express timed at up to the then-magic 100mph.

As I found on a preview run, HSTs were smooth, comfortable and fast, but they lacked the charisma and the aura of majesty and power of the old-style express.

The aim of the *Railway Roundabout* programmes was to inform as well as entertain, and before boarding the 'Bristolian' Bath Road locomotive depot was visited to see final preparations being made. The locomotive, 4-6-0 No 7018 *Drysllwyn Castle*, already had its straight-sided Hawksworth tender piled high with coal. One of the driver's jobs was to 'oil around' while the guard checked the stock formation.

Ten years after Nationalisation, the 'Bristolian' epitomised the spirit of the old Great Western, even though the shining locomotive had been built in 1949 when Swindon works belonged to British Railways. It became, back there in 1956, the first of two of the 'Castle' class to be fitted with a double chimney. The other, No 5043 *Earl of Mount Edgcumbe*, built in 1936, is seen towards the end of this sequence arriving at Paddington with the 'Bristolian' on another day.

The 1958 'Bristolian' was composed of BR standard Mk 1 side-corridor stock, turned out in much-loved GWR chocolate and cream livery, plus an original company dining car where passengers still enjoyed silver service.

The guard wore GWR uniform and the driver had his name on a plate on the cab side. As this was a short-lived innovation of 1958, the programme team was lucky to capture it for posterity.

What a grand sight the 'Bristolian' must have looked in the late afternoon sunshine of a summer's day as it dashed across the Cotswolds via Badminton, having left a wide and curved platform at Temple Meads at half past four. It was allowed 1hr 45min for its journey of almost 118 miles to Paddington, fractionally shorter than Brunel's broad-gauge route via Bath.

Filming was a complex operation which took five days. It involved clamping a camera to the cab side of *Drysllwyn Castle* to get shots showing how rough a footplate could be at high speed, however good the track.

The journey had to be made in midweek because the more powerful 'King' class 4-6-0s were needed on Fridays when the usual, light seven-coach formation was strengthened because so many people were travelling. The 'Bristolian' was always a train of strictly limited stock loading to meet its tight schedules.

The title had a short-lived revival after being restored to timetables in 1972, only to be finally dropped with the introduction of HSTs in 1976. Yet with the 'Cornish Riviera' and the 'Cheltenham Flyer', enthusiasts still revere the 'Bristolian' as part of GWR folklore.

Below:
No 7018 *Drysllwyn Castle* backs down to Reading shed, having just come off a running-in turn in 1960. Built at Swindon in May 1949, No 7018 was one of 30 members of the 'Castle' class to be constructed after Nationalisation; the locomotive was withdrawn in September 1963.
Colour-Rail (BRW1165)

Above right:
'Castle' class 4-6-0 No 7015 *Carn Brae Castle* enters Bristol with the up 'Bristolian' in April 1958. On the left a 'County' class 4-6-0 can also be seen. *C. Hogg/Colour Rail (BRW1248)*

Fishguard Harbour

The crowded decks of the ferry *St David* docking at Fishguard was a reminder that the GWR operated important shipping services. The vessel was actually post-Nationalisation, being completed in 1950. It took the name of a ferry built for the opening of Fishguard harbour in summer 1906 and the establishment of ferry services to Southern Ireland, including the 54 nautical mile crossing to Rosslare — the shortest between Wales and Ireland.

Besides constructing new ports at Rosslare and Fishguard, which displaced Neyland, the GWR and Southern Ireland railway companies built several new railways. The GWR provided a 10½-mile direct line from Clarbeston Road to the new port and built a station alongside the harbour.

Fast boat expresses covered the 261 miles from Paddington in under 6hr, the GWR boasting that the new route 'enables the tourist to breakfast in London and sup on the shores of Killarney's lakes'.

Timings were cut to under 5hr after Cunard liners including the *Lusitania* and *Mauretania*, the largest and fastest vessels in the world, began calling at Fishguard in 1909 to get passengers from New York to London quicker than by any other route.

Restaurant-car boat expresses called only at Cardiff to make connections to and from the Midlands and Northern England. They ceased when Cunard switched trans-Atlantic sailings elsewhere in 1914. Fishguard then reverted to being a busy rail-served ferry port, as it remains today.

When the *Railway Roundabout* film was shot, one of the connecting train services was formed by a portion of the 'Capitals United' express, worked by 'Hall' class 4-6-0 No 5905 *Knowsley Hall*, which was among the small allocation of Fishguard shed, which the GWR had opened with the harbour in 1906.

Expresses, which had to be banked up a stiff gradient on departure, reached Paddington in about 7hr. Timetables warned passengers that up timings were dependent on the arrival of Rosslare and Waterford ferries.

Before the introduction of drive-on-drive-off car ferries, a limited number of motor cars were conveyed by the 'steamers', as they were designated in timetables. Vehicles had to be swung aboard by crane. That practice is shown again in the film of Southampton docks.

Reading
Clark, R. H., *An Historical Survey of Selected Great Western Stations, Volume 2*

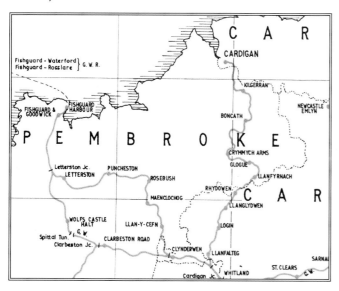

Clarbeston Road–Letterston Junction Cut-Off
Distance: 10½ miles
Owner: Great Western Railway
Opened: 30 August 1906.
Fishguard–Rosslare ferry route inaugurated.

Above:
The 3ft 0in gauge County Donegal Railways Joint Committee operated a network of lines southwest from Strabane to Letterkenny, Glenties, Kilybegs and Ballyshannon. Like part of the Londonderry & Lough Swilly Railway, part of the line of the CDRJC was originally constructed to the Irish standard gauge of 5ft 3in, but was converted to the narrow gauge in the 1890s with the transhipment point to the standard gauge becoming Strabane. The CDRJC was the largest of the Irish narrow gauge systems with a total route mileage of 114 and a steam locomotive allocation of 21. Here, on 2 August 1958, one of the line's locomotives, *Meengilas*, enters Strabane station. *Eric Russell/Colour-Rail*

Irish Narrow Gauge

'With the virtual extinction of the narrow-gauge railway in England and Wales, Ireland has become a place of pilgrimage for the narrow-gauge enthusiast' — the thoughts of L. T. C. (Tom) Rolt in the memorable classic *Lines of Character* which he published with Pat Whitehouse in 1952. Six years later, Pat Whitehouse made a film, equally fascinating, of the dying days of the Irish narrow gauge.

His knowledge — and love — of the remainder of a much decimated system, led him to Ballinamore and Stranorlar. They were the 'last two narrow-gauge railway towns left in these islands', as he described them in *Narrow Gauge Album* (Ian Allan, 1957). By retaining workshops, which could carry out all but the heaviest locomotive repairs, they lay at the heart of the Irish 3ft gauge railways.

Two lines were shown in the sequence: the Cavan & Leitrim section of Coras Iompair Eireann and the County Donegal Railways Joint Committee.

Ballinamore, the largest town on the C&LR, was visited on August Fair day. It was the junction of the 15-mile Drumshambo branch to Arigna, where coal was mined for power stations. The locomotive in charge of a coal train seen running beside a main road was a Hunslet 2-6-2 tank,

No 5T, the T denoting that it once belonged to the Tralee & Dingle Light Railway that had lost its passenger service in 1939 and closed completely in 1953.

Distinctive locomotives added to the appeal of the systems; Ballinamore shed housed veteran 4-4-0 tanks. For years they headed mixed trains on the branch and the 33-mile main line between Belturbet and Dromod.

When the C&LR passed into history in April 1959, Ireland lost its last wholly steam-operated narrow gauge lines.

The end of the same year brought closure of the lines of the County Donegal Railways Joint Committee system which has its headquarters at Stranorlar. Railcars usually handled traffic — the company had eight of them — but because of the Bank Holiday, two steam-hauled specials were substituted for seaside excursions to Ballyshannon.

The Irish narrow gauge was so attractive that even the introduction of railcars failed to dampen the interest of steam enthusiasts, partly because there were highly individual aspects of their operation.

The camera caught one on that bank holiday at Donegal Town. Passengers on a service train so crowded that an ordinary coach was sandwiched between two railcars, stayed in the railcars while they were turned on a manual table. The train was remarshalled with a second coach being attached, this time at the rear, before departing to run through the rugged scenery beside Donegal Bay.

The Joint Committee found railcars attractive because steps allowed them to stop anywhere. But they could not stop the decline. After closure of the system, two were shipped to the Isle of Man where they still run and stir memories for many visitors.

Reading

A number of books are devoted to the Irish narrow gauge lines. Details are also found in Rowledge, J. W. P., *A Regional History of Railways, Volume 16 Ireland.*

Cavan & Leitrim
Distance: 33 miles
Gauge: 3ft
Opened: 1887–88
Closed: 1 April 1959

County Donegal Railways Joint Committee
Strabane–Donegal–Ballyshannon: 46 miles
Gauge: 3ft
Opened: 1889–1905
Closed: 1 January 1960

Right:
The LRTL special of June 1953 is pictured at Dromod station. Cavan & Leitrim No 12L provides the motive power and a suitable headboard has been provided. *J. M. Jarvis/Colour-Rail (NG113)*

Below:
This delightful scene, at Stranorlar on 22 May 1956, sees CDRJC railcar No 10. The CDRJC was an early user of petrol-engined railcars, receiving its first in 1931. A total of 20, the majority built by Walker Bros of Wigan, entered service between then and 1952, taking over most of the passenger services. Two of the later vehicles were eventually to be sold to the Isle of Man, where they are still in service.
Eric Russell/Colour-Rail

Above:
A dramatic scene on the Cavan & Leitrim in June 1953 sees members of the Light Rail Transport League, whose special it was, examining the remains of a Ford 8 hit by C&LR No 3L at Mehanagh Crossing, near Arigna. *J. M. Jarvis/Colour-Rail (NG110)*

Below:
Pictured at Kilturbrid, on the section of the Cavan & Leitrim between Ballinamore and Arigna that opened in 1888, on 6 May 1957 is ex-Tralee & Dingle No 3T. *Colour-Rail*

Camping Coaches

Coaching stock enthusiasts often went in search of holiday camping coaches. They were a familiar sight in 1958 when British Railways had more than 200 scattered on 125 sites throughout England, Scotland and Wales.

Western Region coaches like those in a siding at Gara Bridge, were converted from main line stock to provide sleeping accommodation, a living room and well-equipped kitchen for up to eight people. The coaches were popular because of being comfortable, yet cheap to rent. They were maintained and stored at Swindon in winter and taken to sites in spring and removed each autumn.

How many spotters persuaded mum and dad to take a holiday in them because they were parked beside main and branch lines? A riverside setting made Gara Bridge especially attractive. It was the only passing place and the second of three intermediate stations on the 12½-mile branch from the South Devon main line at Brent to Kingsbridge, which was the railhead for Salcombe.

Holidaymakers at Gara Bridge were assured of a good night's sleep because the first train of the morning did not call until 7.45am and the last departed south at 9pm.

The branch was closed on Sundays, but during the rest of the week the Gara Bridge signalman opened and closed the crossing gates for goods as well as passenger trains. The branch carried quite substantial freight until the complete closure in autumn 1963. It was just 70 years old.

Pat Whitehouse shot this jolly, short film, with the camping coach boys as a willing cast, while he was on holiday. It is historically important as a reminder of an almost forgotten aspect of railway enterprise which met the needs of holidaymakers after World War 2 when accommodation was often hard to find.

Reading
Clark, R. H., *An Historical Survey of Selected Great Western Stations, Volume 2*

Brent–Kingsbridge	
Distance:	12½ miles
Owner:	Great Western Railway
Opened:	1893
Closed:	16 September 1963

Below:
Camping coach No W9906W is captured at Luxulyan on 18 June 1960. This clerestory coach originally dated from 1902 and was converted to a camping coach in 1952. *R. C. Riley*

Bottom:
A later conversion was No W9889W, in 1957, seen at Marazion on 20 April 1961. The 'toplight' coach was constructed to Lot No 1234 in early 1914. *R. C. Riley*

Trains on the Lickey Incline and Operation of the Lickey Incline

In the 1930s, LMS handbills advertised cheap tickets to the 'beautiful Lickey Hills'. That was not a description favoured by staff who had to cope with endless operating problems of the Lickey incline. It is the most famous and only survivor of three stiff, steam-worked, standard gauge inclines captured by *Railway Roundabout* cameras. It was not as steep as the Werneth near Oldham or those on the Cromford & High Peak Railway in Derbyshire, but the Lickey with its straight unbroken 2-mile gradient at 1 in 37.7 was by far the busiest and most spectacular.

Spotters travelled for miles to be banked by 'Big Bertha', an 0-10-0 which the Midland Railway built in 1919, specially for working it. As LMS No 22290 or BR No 58100, it had its own class entry in Ian Allan *abc*s and many spotters still remember the day, at least four decades ago, when they underlined it as a 'prized cop'.

Railway Roundabout did not visit Bromsgrove until about two years after 'Big Bertha' had gone and its big and powerful headlight for night buffering-up had been transferred to a BR standard Class 9F 2-10-0. But there was still plenty to enjoy: long, double-headed expresses stopping short of the station to pick up bankers, ever-active signals raising expectations of the approach of a whole variety of trains or controlling bankers moving in and out of their sidings on the west side of the main line.

The locomotive variety was due partly to the Birmingham and Bristol main line belonging to two regions. After Nationalisation in 1948, the main line passed to the Western

Below:
Class 9F 2-10-0 No 92079 is seen banking No 73028 up the Lickey incline on 12 August 1961 with a Sheffield-bound train. *Eric Russell/Colour-Rail*

Right:
Ex-GWR 0-6-0PT No 8406 and ex-LMS 'Jinty' No 47638 are captured hard at work on the Lickey incline on 20 April 1957. *R. C. Riley*

Below right:
A general view from Bromsgrove on 20 April 1957 shows a freight train approaching the station, having descended the bank, with a 'Jinty' 0-6-0T on the left awaiting its next duty. *R. C. Riley*

Above:
Bromsgrove shed (21C) was located to the south of the station. Originating with the Midland Railway, it was to pass to Western Region control (as 85F between 1958 and 1960 and 85D from 1960 until closure in 1964). For many years the shed was famous as the home of the unique ex-MR 0-10-0 No 58100, but by the date of this photograph, 20 April 1967, 'Big Bertha' had been withdrawn. Visible on shed are two Class 3F 0-6-0s, Nos 43762 and 43186, and a 'Jinty' 0-6-0T. *R. C. Riley*

Region but in February 1958 the section north of Barnt Green, the neighbouring station to Blackwell at the top of the bank, was transferred to the London Midland Region.

An unusual WR representative was a former GWR 2-8-0 tank No 5226. Its presence was short-lived, partly because it did not fit the special power classification given to banking engines. The classification was based on the power of ex-LMS 'Jinty' 0-6-0 tanks and rated 2-10-0s as equal to two tanks.

The Birmingham–Bristol main line was taken over the Lickey Hills rather than round them because of the determination of the promoters of the Birmingham & Gloucester Railway in the 1840s to build the most direct route between those places. A far less severely graded route running to the east was surveyed by Brunel in 1832. Had he been successful, the Birmingham and Bristol main line would have been robbed of its most dramatic interest. Despite the operating handicap of the incline, the Midland Railway, which took over the Birmingham–Bristol in 1846, was still able to exploit it as the 'quickest and most direct route between Birmingham, Bristol, Bath and West of England'.

The time passenger trains occupy the Lickey has changed little over the years. In Victorian days, Midland stopping trains were allowed 12min between Bromsgrove and Blackwell and 9min to descend the bank. Between Nationalisation and April 1964, when Blackwell station closed, an up train was booked 9min and one descending, 4min less. Today timings are little different for trains to and from Birmingham New Street for which Bromsgove is their first or last stop.

Before modernisation, the procession of up and down trains was controlled from Blackwell signalbox at the station.

An intermediate block signal half way up the bank allowed two trains to climb at once — an operation monitored with elaborate equipment. The signalman was also responsible for crossing over banking engines descending to Bromsgrove, travelling in convoy at busy times.

Descending freight trains caused the biggest operating problems because of the variety of their braking powers. Brakes had to be pinned down on every three or four wagons of a semi-fitted train and on every wagon of a loose-coupled freight.

More than a century ago, the historian John Pendleton wrote in *Our Railways, Their Origin, Development, Incident and Romance*, of the advantages there would have been if a different route had been built. He noted: 'The incline is not without a spice of danger; the cost of it in waste, inconvenience and loss of time would probably have constructed a level line, and yielded a big profit, but the Lickey works on still'.

Reading
Casserley, H. C., *The Lickey Incline*
Preston Hendry, Dr R. & Powell Hendry, R., *An Historical Survey of Selected LMS Stations, Volume 2*

ahead of complete closure between Halesowen and Longbridge West via Rubery, the only crossing place.

Today, the first ¾-mile of the branch from the Birmingham & Bristol main line at Halesowen Junction, Longbridge, is busy with car-carrying trains which load in sidings of what are now the Rover works.

Enthusiasts remember the branch as a line of character, partly because Halesowen lay at the foot of steep banks on which some trains in both directions needed bankers. It was also a line where in later years the LMS used veteran Midland locomotives including Kirtley double-frame 0-6-0s, and the GWR half-cab 0-6-0 pannier tanks and four-wheel coaches.

Reading
Hale M., & Williams, N., *By Rail to Halesowen*

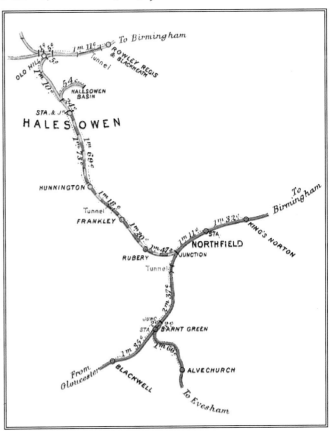

The Halesowen Branch

Millions of cars and lorries cross the grave of the GWR and Midland Railway branch from Longbridge to Halesowen, for the six-lane M5 bisects its buried trackbed near the first overbridge spanning the motorway south of Frankley Services.

This was the second of two railways to Halesowen. The GWR opened a single branch from its Stourbridge line at Old Hill, 1½ miles north, in 1878 and five years later made an end-on junction with the 6-mile Halesowen Railway built by a private company from Longbridge. In 1906 ownership was transferred to the GWR and Midland Joint.

The film, shot on the Joint line rather than on the GWR branch, provides a last record of one of the most distinctive railway landmarks in the West Midlands. The footplate of a Bournville-based ex-Midland '2F' 0-6-0 is the grandstand for impressive shots of the 100ft-high trestle-built Dowery Dell viaduct.

The branch was interesting for the nature of its passenger services. Public timetable services between Halesowen, Longbridge and Northfield of five weekday trains each way, ended in April 1919. Six years later the GWR withdrew its Halesowen–Old Hill railcar service in 1927. But the branch continued to carry heavily loaded workmen's trains, not shown in ordinary timetables, to and from the Austin motor works at Longbridge. They ended in autumn 1958, six years

Halesowen Branches

Old Hill–Halesowen
Distance: 1½ miles
Owner: Great Western Railway
Opened: 1878. Halesowen Canal Basin branch 1902
Closed: 5 December 1927 Regular passenger services
1 September 1958 Old Hill–Longbridge workmen's specials
1 October 1969 Old Hill–Halesowen Canal Basin completely

Halesowen–Longbridge West
Distance: 6 miles
Owner: GWR and Midland Joint
Opened: 1883
Closed: April 1919 Halesowen–Longbridge–Northfield. Midland Railway regular passenger services.
1 September 1958 Old Hill–Longbridge workmen's specials
6 January 1964 Halesowen–Rubery completely

Hayling Island Branch

Diminutive 'Terrier' tanks pulling mixed trains of elderly coaches and wagons across a long wooden viaduct; locomotive smoke evaporating in gentle summer breezes or being snatched away by winter gales. Such were the joys of the 4½-mile Hayling Island branch in later years.

Construction was slow for although a local company, the Hayling Railway, was authorised in 1860 to build a branch from the London Brighton & South Coast main line at Havant, to the Island, it was not fully opened until 1867. There were difficulties in building a wooden trestle viaduct across the busy tidal waters of Langston harbour.

The initiative for completion came from a wealthy London businessman, Francis Fuller, who went on holiday and immediately realised that a resort could be developed. He revived the almost moribund project and became chairman of the Hayling Railway. An admiral was one of its other three directors.

Five years after completion of the single line with two intermediate stations but no passing place, it was leased to

Above:
Stroudley-designed 'Terrier' No 32650 is caught at the diminutive station of North Hayling on 8 September 1962. R. C. Riley

Left:
'Terrier' No 32662 (originally London, Brighton & South Coast No 62 Martello) is seen with a two-coach train crossing Langston Viaduct in August 1963. This locomotive is now preserved and today can be seen at Bressingham.
J. A. C. Kirke/Colour-Rail

the LB&SCR, with the small company retaining its independence. This was to last until it became part of the Southern Railway in 1923.

The year 1872 was also important in the line's history for it marked the introduction by William Stroudley of his 'Terrier' tanks. Because they weighed only 27½ tons, they were ideal for working across the trestle viaduct.

By the 1950s, the branch was one of the few in Britain on which mixed trains were still allowed and they sometimes formed the 14 workings — on weekdays in winter and daily in summer. A journey over the single line took 13min.

Five 'Terriers' were still working the branch in the late 1950s, and while several have been preserved, No 32661 was later scrapped. It was one of the 'A1x' class of 'Terriers' rebuilt with extended smokeboxes. Its chimney-spark arrester was a legacy from the days when it worked on the Newhaven Harbour branch.

The 'Terriers' worked the line for nearly 70 years pulling trains which carried holidaymakers in their thousands. Around the turn of the century, Baedeker guides noted that from Havant 'a short branch line diverges to Hayling Island,

with the favourite bathing resorts of North and South Hayling'.

Tourists attracted by his comments would have completed their journeys there by 'Terriers'. After closure most of the branch was converted into a coastal path. The viaduct was dismantled.

Reading
Smith, M., *British Railway Bridges and Viaducts*, Ian Allan Publishing

Havant–Hayling Island	
Distance:	4½ miles
Owner:	London Brighton & South Coast Railway
Opened:	1867
Closed:	4 November 1963

Below:
Built in 1880 and rebuilt in 1911, No 32678 was already more than 80 years old when photographed at North Hayling on 29 July 1962. Originally LBSCR No 78 *Knowle*, this is another member of the class to survive in preservation and today can be seen at Tenterden on the Kent & East Sussex Railway. *J. P. Mullett/Colour-Rail*

Above:
This delightful study of a long-lost line sees
'Terrier' No 32650 near Langston on
2 November 1963. This locomotive, originally
London, Brighton & South Coast Railway No 50
Sutton, was built in 1876 and withdrawn shortly
after the date of this photograph. Now also
preserved, the locomotive can be seen on the Kent
& East Sussex Railway. *R. C. Riley*

Left:
Pictured on Hayling Island on 23 August 1959,
'Terrier' No 32640 appears diminutive compared
to its two-coach train. Built in March 1878 as
LBSCR No 40 *Brighton*, the locomotive was sold
to the Isle of Wight Central Railway in January
1902, becoming IoWCR No 11 before becoming
SR No W11 *Newport* in 1923. It returned to the
mainland in 1947, being renumbered 2640 and
again to No 32640 in 1948. No 32640 was
withdrawn in September 1963 and was initially
preserved at the Butlin's holiday camp at Pwllheli;
more recently the locomotive has been transferred
back to the Isle of Wight and is now based on the
steam railway there. *Chris Gammell*

The Southwell Branch

Part of the appeal of the *Railway Roundabout* series stemmed from the variety of veteran locomotives it showed at work. The Southwell branch in Nottinghamshire was one of the last haunts of neat 0-4-4 tanks which Johnson introduced on the Midland Railway in 1881. No 58085 was working the one-coach push and pull service connecting with Nottingham–Newark–Lincoln services at Rolleston Junction, where the station was an attractive legacy of the Midland Railway. The 'Southwell Paddy' waited in the bay platform and contrast of motive power, often found during the modernisation programme begun in the mid-1950s, was provided when a Lincoln-bound service was formed of an early DMU.

Once again, filming was timely for the scene was soon to change. The 2½-mile nonstop service, booked to take 5min, was withdrawn in summer 1959 and No 58085 scrapped the following year.

The 'Paddy' ran about 12 times each way on weekdays only from quite early in the morning until early evening with the last departure from Rolleston about 7pm. After it was withdrawn, the branch remained open for freight until the mid-1960s.

The line between Rolleston and Southwell was opened purely as a branch in 1847 and did not lose that status until the line was extended 12 miles north in the 1870s to meet another Midland Railway branch near Mansfield.

Above:
Ex-Midland Railway 0-4-4T No 58065 is seen at Southwell on 4 April 1959. By this date No 58065 was one of only three of the type still in service. More than 200 of these tanks were built for the Midland to a design of Johnson between 1875 and 1900. No 58065 was built in 1892 as MR No 2019. It was renumbered 1367 in 1907 and in 1925 it was rebuilt with a Belpaire firebox. It was to be withdrawn in October 1959. The last of the surviving trio was withdrawn in August 1960. *C. H. Hunt/Colour-Rail*

Until 1929, three weekday-only trains linked Mansfield and Newark, serving five local stations including Southwell and Rolleston Junction. Specials to Southwell racecourse adjacent to Rolleston, and excursions to the Lincolnshire coast were routed over the branch, but its most important traffic was from collieries near Mansfield. The volume of traffic led the LMS to double between Southwell and Rolleston, where a south spur was built to allow through-running west towards Nottingham.

Enthusiasts wanting to recall the line can follow the 6-mile Southwell Trail along the trackbed north from the town, famed for its Minster.

Reading
Vinter, J. *Railway Walks*. LMS
Trains Illustrated, June 1958, 'Snapshot of the Southwell Branch'

Rolleston Junction–Southwell	
Distance:	2½ miles
Owner:	Midland Railway
Opened:	1847
Closed:	15 June 1959 for Passengers
	7 December 1964 for Goods

The 'Rother Valley Limited'

'Terrier' tanks 'topped and tailed' a special train run over the then remaining 13½ miles of the Kent & East Sussex Railway between Robertsbridge and Tenterden in October 1958. It was crowded with enthusiasts who were passengers on the Locomotive Club of Great Britain 'Rother Valley Limited'. The main train, composed of straight-sided Hasting coaches, arrived at Robertsbridge from London behind Class E 4-4-0 No 31019, a Maunsell rebuild of a Wainwright design of 1905.

The K&ES was authorised in 1896 as the Rother Valley Light Railway. The engineer was Colonel Holman Stephens who became managing director in 1900, three years ahead of the opening of the first section between Robertsbridge and Tenterden. The Railway Clearing House coloured its 21½-mile route in dark blue in contrast to pink chosen for South Eastern & Chatham lines which it linked.

The K&ES went into receivership in 1932, by which time it was 'more of a resort for rail fans than of any economic importance' according to Professor Pat White in his *Regional History of Railways*.

Despite financial and other problems, the independent company was absorbed into BR at Nationalisation and the sparse services were improved. The strategy was not successful and early in 1954, passenger services were withdrawn and the eight miles between Tenterden and Headcorn closed completely.

After shuttling back to Robertsbridge the 'Rother Valley Limited' continued to Bexhill West and Newhaven and then ran to Victoria — a London terminus from which there were never any trains connecting with either terminal of the K&ES.

It was not the only passenger train to run over the Rother Valley section in 1958 for summer hop-pickers' specials to Bodiam continued until the following year.

Freight services survived until 1961 when preservationists became active and today the K&ES is once again independent and back in public timetables, with the 7-mile preserved line between Tenterden and Northiam listed among Private Railway Companies. A trip over it introduced me to a Kent which until then I had seen mainly from Continental boat trains and got to know through the writings of Siegfried Sassoon, who immortalised the railways of the Weald in poetry.

Reading
Smith, M., *Britain's Light Railways*, Ian Allan Publishing

Robertsbridge–Headcorn
Distance:	21½ miles
Owner:	Kent & East Sussex Light Railway
Opened:	1900–1905
Closed:	2 January 1954 for Passengers. Tenterden–Headcorn completely. 12 June 1961 Robertsbridge–Tenterden for Goods.
Reopened:	Kent & East Sussex Steam Railway between Tenterden and Northiam.

Below:
The 'Rother Valley Limited' was brought to Robertsbridge behind 'E1' class 4-4-0 No 31019. It is seen here on arrival at Robertsbridge on 19 October 1958. *Eric Russell/Colour-Rail*

Above:
One of the two 'Terriers' used for the 'Rother Valley Limited' was the Brighton Works shunter No DS377. It had been repainted into an authentic LBSCR livery for that role and looked attractive at the head of the train at Rolvenden. No DS377, as LBSCR No 35 *Morden*, dated back to June 1878; it was transferred to service stock in 1946. After its career at Brighton Works, it was reinstated to capital stock before final withdrawal in March 1963. Unlike a number of other class members, No DS377 was not to survive into preservation.
Eric Russell/Colour-Rail

Below:
The second of the two 'Terriers' used to 'top and tail' the special was No 32678, which we have already encountered four years later on the Hayling Island branch, from where it was withdrawn in 1963. It is seen here at Robertsbridge heading into the station from the K&ESR line. This section of line was closed in 1961, although a short section to Hodson's siding was retained officially until 1970 (a landslip caused its actual closure the previous year). If current proposals succeed, the preserved Kent & East Sussex Railway could once again provide a link to this point.
Eric Russell/Colour-Rail

Southampton Docks

'Most of our lives we are either seeking business or pleasure. Let the Southampton Docks be your gateway to both.' That 'au revoir' by the unnamed author of a Southern Railway souvenir brochure of the early 1930s, set a mood which John Adams captured over a quarter of a century later in a 6min film which completed the *Railway Roundabout* video of 1958.

Among the biggest changes in nearly four decades since then has been the decline of the railway-owned dock railway system, one of the largest in Britain. Its most distinctive feature after World War 2 was a fleet of USA 0-6-0 shunting tanks, or 'switchers' as the crews of American ships berthed nearby would have known them if they were rail buffs.

Bought as Government surplus after the war, their short wheelbases, easy maintenance and good power made them ideal for shunting operations. An innovation was movement control by a two-way radio link between control and the locomotives using sets installed in their cabs.

The tanks were listed in Ian Allan Publishing's *abcs* as British Railways locomotives carrying the numbers 30060–74 of Class USA. Four of the 14 have been preserved. How different the railway scene would be today if so high a proportion of all steam classes had survived!

Scrapping was the fate of two former London Brighton & South Coast 0-6-0 tanks of SR Classes E1 and E2, which still shunted the sidings a decade after Nationalisation, and also several classes of main line steam locomotives which handled ocean liner expresses between London and the port.

Ocean liner expresses, often carrying statesmen and film stars, and the liners in which they sailed, provided the glamorous background against which the dock shunters worked.

'Lord Nelson' class 4-6-0s monopolised expresses carrying passengers arriving or sailing in the Cunarders *Queen Elizabeth* and *Queen Mary* which maintained weekly sailings between Southampton and New York. Cunard ocean liner expresses were made up of Pullman cars rather than standard coaches. Pullmans were also used on boat trains for other large liners.

The 'Queens' berthed at Southampton Ocean Terminal, a striking precast concrete two-storey building nearly a quarter of a mile long with an island platform which accommodated two full-length boat trains. It was officially opened in summer 1950 by the Prime Minister, Clement Attlee.

Streamlined 'Battle of Britain' class Pacifics headed regular Channel Island boat trains made up of standard corridor stock, which used a station inside a dock warehouse.

The Ocean Terminal was demolished after the 'Queens' ended the trans-Atlantic service, beaten by the introduction of the big jet airliners in the late 1950s.

Viewing
Ocean Terminal (British Transport Films [undated]) is a splendid evocation of the Southampton port scene in the late 1950s. It shows the dock shunters, freight trains and banana specials run from the docks to destinations all over the country; ocean liner expresses; the Ocean Terminal and the two 'Queen' liners. This film is occasionally shown on TV.

Below:
Seen alongside the Ocean Terminal at Southampton is 'Lord Nelson' 4-6-0 No 30857 *Lord Howe* awaiting departure with 'The Cunarder' service to Waterloo. *Colour-Rail (BRS995)*

Above right:
A second 'Lord Nelson', No 30861 *Lord Anson*, is pictured at Nine Elms with the 'Holland American' headboard. *Colour-Rail*

Below right:
One of the 'USA' 0-6-0-Ts allocated to Southampton Docks traffic, No DS233, is seen at the Ocean Terminal on 9 June 1964 with the bow of the Cunard liner *Queen Elizabeth* forming an appropriate backdrop. Following the *Queen's* withdrawal from passenger service, the great liner was eventually to be destroyed by fire in Hong Kong Harbour; sister ship the *Queen Mary* is currently based in California, although her future has been the subject of much debate. *Colour-Rail*

Class B17 4-6-0 No 61652 departs from Cambridge with the 9.50am service to London King's Cross on 22 June 1958. *R. C. Riley*

1959

Great Eastern 'E4' at Cambridge

Among my many memories of ex-Great Eastern 2-4-0s at work in East Anglia in 1948, none is stronger than of a day on which there was a mass exodus of hundreds of personnel from RAF Central Signals Establishment at Watton on the Thetford–Swaffham branch.

The RAF notified the recently-Nationalised British Railways that hundreds of airmen would be going on home leave so that the early afternoon train to the main line at Thetford could be strengthened.

But it was the usual Class E4 and three ancient GER coaches that pulled into a jammed platform. The coaches got so packed that it was impossible to see if anyone was left behind. But I was envious of two airmen who were invited to ride on the footplate.

Delay in loading at Watton was made up on the nine miles of the branch through rural Norfolk to Roundham Junction on the main line and the following four miles to Thetford, where a sea of blue uniforms awaited the next express to London. That was not due into Liverpool Street until well over three hours later.

The 'E4s' — as the LNER classified these sturdy locomotives — were the last 2-4-0s to work in Britain. Known to Great Eastern men as 'intermediates', 100 were built to the design of James Holden between 1891 and 1902.

Branch line work was only a retirement duty because for years they were in charge of the Great Eastern's principal expresses. In the Company's Official Guide an 'E4' was shown hauling an express on the 'Cathedrals Route' — Cambridge, Lincoln, Doncaster and York. That was in 1900 — the year Holden introduced his more famous and most beautiful design, the 'Claude Hamilton' 4-4-0s, which displaced the 2-4-0s on express work.

The ranks of the 'E4s' were depleted gradually. A total of 82 had been scrapped by 1940, but my log book of the mid-1940s records sightings of four of the remaining 18 which survived into the 1950s. This was partly because their light weight of only 40 tons gave them wide route availability. In later years after Grouping, they worked over Stainmore Summit between Darlington and Penrith.

No 62785 was withdrawn in 1959 and restored at Stratford works as close as possible to her 1895 condition when she joined the GER locomotive fleet as No 490. That is how she is found in the National Collection at York.

The last passenger train called at Watton in summer 1964. The history of the branch lines to Thetford was told by B. D. J. Walsh in *The Railway Magazine*, June 1953 — 11 years before the withdrawal of passenger trains to Swaffham.

Below:
Ex-Great Eastern Railway 2-4-0 No 62785 is captured at Cambridge on 16 May 1959. This was the last survivor of the once 100-strong class designed by Holden. *Colour-Rail*

Above right:
Two months later, on 15 July 1959, No 62785 is seen again at Cambridge; by this time the locomotive was rapidly approaching the end of its operation career. Following withdrawal, No 62785, the last main line 2-4-0 to remain in service, was preserved. Cambridge shed (31A) was to close to steam in June 1962 with its remaining locomotives being transferred to either March or Stratford. *Colour-Rail*

Below right:
Pictured on the turntable at Cambridge shed on 23 June 1958 is Gresley 'A4' Pacific No 60017 *Silver Fox*. *R. C. Riley*

The Closing of the Wye Valley Lines

In an article headed 'Rush Hour at Monmouth Troy' in *Trains Illustrated* in 1953, Marcus Newman wrote: 'Any enthusiast depressed by the continuing spate of British branch line closures should pay a visit to the two-platform station of Monmouth (Troy). At this focal point of three branches, from Chepstow, Ross-on-Wye and Pontypool Road, there are admittedly long periods of drowsy inactivity every day, but this is because throughout most of the day the services on the three branches are scheduled to connect with each other at Monmouth (Troy). Three times a day the station hums with sudden life as all three little trains bustle in, one after the other.'

Monmouth Troy had not always been a station where passengers had to change. Before World War 1, passenger and goods traffic was heavy enough for the GWR to run passenger and mixed trains between Ross, Monmouth and Pontypool Road. The through journey, with a 4min wait at Troy, took 1hr 25min.

Monmouth–Pontypool Road passenger trains were withdrawn in summer 1955 reducing the bustle found by Marcus Newman at Troy station. It disappeared altogether when the Ross and Chepstow branches were closed three and a half years later.

The railways had done all they could to encourage traffic. The GWR opened a string of little halts and, in 1938, published a full-length guide for ramblers. Only a year later, the GWR had to stick red labels on the title page warning ramblers that because of wartime conditions, some walks shown in the guide might no longer be open.

Britain was still recovering from the war with food still rationed, when I stayed at Ross in summer 1949. Many tourists had returned to the area, but few were travelling on the Wye Valley motor trains.

The running of almost empty trains was among problems faced by the Western Region after Nationalisation. It was reviewed at a Transport Users' Consultative Committee inquiry into proposals made in 1958 to close the Monmouth branches.

Committee members described it as the most controversial and difficult hearing of the year. But they concluded 'with regret' that any hardship caused to local people or the tourist industry was outweighed by the wider economic issue.

So when 1959 was only a few days old, the Ross and Chepstow branch passenger services were withdrawn. The Ross branch remained open to freight until 1964–65 and also retained for mineral traffic was the first mile of the Monmouth branch from Wye Valley Junction to Tidenham stone quarry.

The passenger service economies were marked by a railtour run on 4 January by the Midland area of the Stephenson Locomotive Society. It had its own sense of poignancy because it was the first the Society organised in its Golden Jubilee year. The sense of loss was reflected in a black-edged brochure, which is remembered as a hallmark for such occasions.

John Adams and Pat Whitehouse did not film the special, preferring, as did many enthusiasts at that time, to make farewell trips on the last day of normal passenger services.

The short winter day produced a good illustration of the problems in making the *Railway Roundabout* films; it was impossible to film the last departure of the day from Monmouth because the light had gone.

Reading
Page, James, *Forgotten Railways: South Wales*

Wye Valley Branches

Little Mill Junction–Monmouth (Troy)
Distance: 15 miles
Opened: 1856–57
Closed: 30 May 1955 Pontypool Road–Little Mill Junction–Monmouth (Troy) for Passengers
13 June 1955 Usk–Monmouth (Troy) for Goods
13 September 1965 Glascoed–Usk for Goods

Ross-on-Wye–Monmouth (Troy)
Distance: 13 miles
Opened: 1873–74
Closed: 5 January 1959 Ross–Monmouth (Troy) for Passengers
2 November 1964 Monmouth (Troy)–Lydbrook for Goods
1 November 1965 Lydbrook–Ross-on-Wye for Goods

Chepstow (Wye Valley Junction)–Monmouth (Troy)
Distance: 13 miles
Opened: 1861–1876
Closed: 5 January 1959 Chepstow (Wye Valley Junction)–Monmouth (Troy) for Passengers
6 January 1964 Tidenham Quarry–Monmouth (Troy) for Goods

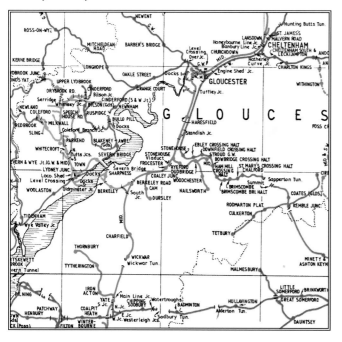

Right:
The SLS-sponsored tour of 4 January 1959 makes its way through appropriately wintry weather up the Wye Valley. *Colour-Rail*

Below:
On 4 January 1959 ex-GWR 0-6-0PT No 6439 is pictured at Ross-on-Wye with the SLS-organised special that operated over the Wye Valley lines to mark the closure of the route. *W. Potter/Colour-Rail*

SLS Special to Harborne

There is far more variety to this film than the title suggests. Viewing the 1959 video for the first time I was surprised to find that it included the Halesowen branches seen already in 1958. Yet this journey added fresh interest to a branch, which, like Harborne, was under threat of final closure. Three Midland tender 0-6-0s of ancient appearance even four decades ago were seen at different locations on a wide-ranging SLS Birmingham area railtour.

Equally nostalgic were some of the cameras used to photograph it. One enthusiast — or was he a press photographer? — carried a heavy plate camera fitted with a large flashgun. He recorded the departure from Birmingham New Street of the special, topped and tailed by 0-6-0s, as it passed a 'Jubilee' class 4-6-0.

The curtain-raiser of the tour was a run over the Harborne branch which would have joined the Halesowen line at Lapel had the early promoters had their way. Instead, the branch terminated at a charming suburban station in the centre of Harborne from which the LNWR ran more than 40 trains a day to and from New Street.

Finding paths for them over the congested Stour Valley route must have been an operator's nightmare, something akin to piecing together the famous and scarce wooden GWR jigsaws made at the Chad Valley toy factory served by the Harborne line.

Between Harborne and Halesowen, old and new forms of traction were filmed within sight of each other at Smethwick Junction. As the railtour approached, a Western Region three-car DMU took the Birmingham Snow Hill route, reopened as the Jewellery Line in 1995.

The special reached Halesowen from Old Hill, which was unusual because only WR pannier tanks ran through between Old Hill and Longbridge. Workings from Longbridge terminated at Halesowen.

The withdrawal of workmen's trains between Old Hill and Longbridge in autumn 1958 ended passenger economies begun in 1919 with the withdrawal of a Midland and GW joint service. Edwardian *Bradshaw's* showed five trains with first and third class accommodation, running each way between Halesowen and King's Norton on the Birmingham–Bristol main line — a total distance of $8\frac{1}{4}$ miles.

An unusual legacy of the GWR withdrawal of Old Hill–Halesowen local services in 1927 was left in the company's *Holiday Haunts* guides in which there was a substantial entry about the attractions of Halesowen. A note reminded tourists that there was a substitute weekday GWR Road Motor Service.

Reading and viewing
Hale, M. & Williams, N., *By Rail to Halesowen*
Railway Roundabout video 1958

Harborne Branch

Harborne Junction–Harborne
Distance: 2½ miles
Owner: London & North Western Railway
Opened: 1874
Closed: 26 November 1934 for Passengers
4 November 1963 for Goods

Below:
Ex-Midland Railway Class 2F 0-6-0 No 58283 is pictured at Harborne with the SLS special on 30 May 1959. Note in the foreground the crouching figure of John Adams with his camera. *Eric Russell/Colour-Rail*

Above right:
A second ex-Midland Railway '2F' 0-6-0, No 58271, is seen at Monument Lane. This shed was situated on the ex-LNWR main line just west of New Street station. At the time of the *Railway Roundabout* recording, the shed was coded 3E, but in 1960 it was to become 21E; it was closed in 1962. By this time rapid inroads were being made into the numbers of these 0-6-0s. No 58271 was built as MR No 2306 by Neilson & Co in 1896; it was renumbered 3492 in 1907 and retained that number at the Grouping in 1923. It was finally withdrawn in May 1961. *John Adams/Colour-Rail*

Below right:
Suitably bulled up for this duty Class 2F 0-6-0 No 58271 is seen again, this time heading along the Harborne branch in May 1959 with an SLS-organised special. The ex-LNWR branch was to close completely five years later, on 4 May 1964. *T. J. Edgington/Colour-Rail*

Midland Compound No 1000

As a boy I hated going to the family dentist until his son invited me to see his model railway in a large attic. Pride of his gauge O double track main line was 4-4-0 No 1185, which Hornby classed as No 2 Special LMS Compound.

I remember it — and my friend who I have not met for 50 years — when I see Midland Compound No 1000 in the National Railway Museum. 'It makes one think more cheerfully of human life', as the writer Nathaniel Hawthorn wrote about the Lake District.

Viewing the Compound at York provides a continuity thread through years of locomotive memories. I remember them best as the film shows BR No 41000 at Crewe Works — black with grime! I used to see them like that at Crewe, Liverpool and along the North Wales coast on the Chester & Holyhead. But they probably never ran as hard on this main line as they did handling 2hr Euston–Birmingham expresses.

While working on BBC radio programmes about railways, I met John Scholes, curator at the Museum of British Transport at Clapham, and I admired his vision and practical approach to the acquisition of a national collection of locomotives.

The early place which No 1000 gained in the collection may have been due to the Compounds having many admirers among professional railwaymen. It was significant that while modernisation was being carried out on a massive scale throughout BR, the locomotive was stored at Crewe for several years before going to Derby for restoration.

When George Dow published *British Steam Horses* in 1950, nearly all of the 240 Compounds built by the Midland and LMS were still at work. He regarded them as S. W. Johnson's greatest masterpiece and as being 'the most handsome of all British 4-4-0s'.

Reading
Graebe, C. and J., *The Hornby Gauge O System*
See also: Publications of the National Railway Museum. Logs of Compound workings are recorded in a number of books about locomotives.

Below:
A view of the Midland Compound at its birthplace on 27 September 1959. Designed by Johnson and built at Derby, as MR No 2631, in January 1902, the locomotive was renumbered to 1000 in 1907 before being rebuilt to Deeley's specification in 1914. It became LMS No 1000 in 1923 and No 41000 at Nationalisation in 1948. Withdrawn in November 1951 and preserved, the locomotive was restored to as near 1914 condition as practical during 1959 and reinstated for use on specials. The lomotive remains part of the National Collection and today is displayed at York. *R. C. Riley*

Above right:
The famous first run of the newly-restored ex-Midland Railway Compound No 1000 sees the locomotive in pristine condition at Rugby Central with the East Midlander railtour in September 1959. *K. C. H. Fairey/Colour-Rail*

Below right:
The ex-Midland Compound is captured entering Derby on an SLS special on 27 September 1959. *R. C. Riley*

Scottish Historical Locomotives

Grouping robbed the railways of Britain of a lot of individuality. Modernisation which followed Nationalisation, devastated it. A glimpse of how much was lost in Scotland is illustrated in this film of its preserved locomotives.

The *Roundabout* team seized a marvellous opportunity to recapture some of the glory of Scottish railways when the locomotives paraded in Glasgow in 1959 as the Scottish Industries Exhibition was being held at the Kelvin Hall. The veterans, based on the former Dawsholm shed of the Caledonian Railway, also hauled a number of special trains in connection with the Exhibition.

Locomotives of four pre-Grouping companies took part: the Caledonian, Great North of Scotland, Highland and North British. The only absentee was a veteran of the Glasgow & South Western, whose locomotives were immortalised in the tales of David L. Smith of Ayr. Also on parade was a 'foreigner': *City of Truro*, the GWR 4-4-0 which is now in the National Collection at York. To reach Glasgow it travelled further north than it had ever been.

Two of the veterans have special claims to fame: Caledonian No 123 was the last 4-2-2 in service in Britain, not being withdrawn until 1935, and the 'Jones Goods' of the Highland Railway of 1894 was the first 4-6-0 to run in Britain. Some of the class of 15 locomotives outlived the single-wheeler, not being withdrawn from service until 1940.

I fell under the spell of Scottish railways in the late 1940s, finding that they had a fascination of their own, difficult to define yet very real. This lingers to some extent on its preserved railways. Both the Bo'ness & Kinneil Railway beside the Forth near Edinburgh, and the Strathspey Railway in the Highlands have atmospheres that are different from those south of the Border.

In 1996 when plans were announced to raise funds to restore the North British 4-4-0 *Glen Douglas* for main line running, I recalled riding behind it in the Borders on part of a Railway Correspondence & Travel Society railtour on a glorious summer day in 1961.

Starting from Leeds, it reached the Borders via the Settle & Carlisle line and ran over the Waverley route to St Boswells and, after visiting the Greenlaw and Jedburgh branches, reached the East Coast main line at Tweedmouth. A tour of more than 400 miles was completed by a return journey to Leeds via Ripon.

Reading
Nock, O. S., *Scottish Railways*

Below:
Designed by Reid and introduced in 1913, 32 of the 'Glen' class 4-4-0s were built between then and 1920. NBR No 256 *Glen Douglas* was the third of the class to be built, emerging from Cowlairs Works in September 1913. It became LNER Class D34 No 9256 at the Grouping, being renumbered 2469 in 1946. As BR No 62469 the locomotive was repainted in NBR livery in August 1959, being officially withdrawn in December 1962 (the last of the class to succumb). Although withdrawn, the locomotive remained available to haul specials until 1965 when it was transferred to the Museum of Transport. It is now based at Bo'ness. It is pictured here at Auchtermuchty, on the Ladybank-Kinross branch, on 17 June 1960 with a joint SLS/RCTS special. *Chris Gammell*

Above:
The fourth of the Scottish pre-Grouping designs to be restored to original livery was ex-Highland Railway 4-6-0 No 103, which is pictured at Blair Atholl on 15 June 1960. This locomotive is also now displayed at the Glasgow Museum of Transport. *Chris Gammell*

Right:
The unique Caledonian Single, No 123, is pictured at Haymarket shed on 12 June 1960. Built in1886 by Neilson & Co, the locomotive was exhibited at the Edinburgh International Exhibition of that year alongside No 124, where it was awarded a gold medal. No 123 was to achieve fame during the first of the 'Railway Races to the North' in 1888. It was renumbered to the duplicate list in 1914 (as No 1123) becoming LMS No 14010 at the Grouping. Withdrawn in April 1935 as the last 4-2-2 in service, the locomotive was preserved and can now be seen in the Glasgow Museum of Transport.
Chris Gammell

Lower right:
Appointed in 1914, T. E. Heywood was to be the Great North of Scotland Railway's last Locomotive Superintendent. Eight 4-4-0s, designated Class F by the GNoSR, were built by North British (six) and Inverurie Works (two) in 1920/21. These superheated locomotives were effectively a development of a Pickersgill design of 1899 and the LNER designated both as Class D40. No 49 *Gordon Highlander* was one of the NB-built examples. It was to be withdrawn in 1958 prior to being repainted in GNoSR livery and is seen restored at Auchterless, on the Macduff branch, on 13 June 1960 with a joint SLS/RCTS special. The locomotive can today be seen in the Glasgow Museum of Transport.
Chris Gammell

The Skye Line: Fort William to Mallaig

'I doubt if there could be found an equal length of railway line in the whole world more crowded with continuous interest... I do hope that some day it will be possible for the LNER to run open coaches with large windows between Glasgow and Mallaig.'

So wrote R. Barnard Way in his rather unusual book *Famous British Trains* — unusual because of his chatty writing. It was published in 1936 when the Fort William–Mallaig extension of the West Highland Line was only 35 years old. It had been completed in spring 1901, a few weeks after the death of Queen Victoria. The 42-mile route is among the youngest and most remote seen on the videos. It is still possible to enjoy virtually the same journey as that shot by John and Pat in May 1959, simply by catching one of the steam-hauled specials run in summer as tourist attractions.

The excursions carry only passengers and the work is a little less arduous for locomotive crews than it was in the heyday of steam when trains often had up to three fish vans attached to the rear. Catches landed by small fishing boats at Mallaig were often heavy enough for special fish trains to be needed.

The video shows one in charge of a Gresley K2 'Mogul'. On stretches where the single track runs close to the sea, their sharply beating exhausts mingled with the cries of the gulls.

The West Highland extension had a strong nautical flavour which found its way into *Bradshaw's*. In Edwardian days, they noted that the running of the 7.20am from Mallaig — the first of the two daily services to Glasgow Queen Street (High Level) — 'is contingent upon the arrival of the steamer from Stornoway'.

When the West Highland Railway opened to Fort William in 1894, the unnamed writer of *Mountain Moor and Loch* (which is now regarded as a classic Victorian guidebook), referred to 'these days of luxurious locomotion'. He claimed that a traveller was carried from London into the heart of the Highlands with almost as little exertion as if he was going from the city to his suburban home.

So far as exertion is concerned, that may have been true, but not as regards the length or speed of journey. Once the extension opened, an 8.15pm departure from King's Cross gave a next-day arrival in Mallaig at 1.45pm. In 1996, a 21.30 departure from Euston offered a 13.20 arrival at Mallaig for ferries to Skye and Stornoway.

Reading
Ellis, C. Hamilton, *The North British Railway*

Fort William–Mallaig

Distance: 41¾ miles
Owner: North British Railway
Opened: 1 April 1901

Above:
The railway at Mallaig boasted impressive facilities, as befitted its role as a rail head for the Western Isles and for the local fishing industry. In this view, taken on 26 September 1963, the new order is already making itself felt with the appearance of a Type 2 diesel-electric No D5367 in the station. *Neil Caplan*

Right:
Sister locomotive, No 61789 with its Eastfield allocation prominent on the front buffer beam, stands at Mallaig in May 1959. Another of the 20 'K2/2s' fitted with side-window cabs, No 61789 was new in July 1921 also from Kitson & Co. The locomotive was destined to end its days away from the West Highland line, being withdrawn from Keith shed in May 1960.
Eric Russell/Colour-Rail

Left:
With the splendours of Loch Linnhe and the 1,531ft peak of Meall t-Slamain forming a suitable backdrop, Gresley-design 'K2/2' 2-6-0 No 61784 awaits departure from Fort William station on 9 May 1959. This was one of 20 of the class to be fitted with side-window cabs for use on Scottish Region metals. The locomotive was originally built as Great Northern Railway No 1694 by Kitson & Co in July 1921. It became No 4694 at the Grouping and was renumbered 1784 in the LNER's 1946 renumbering. It was withdrawn from Fort William shed in March 1961. *Colour-Rail*

The 'Brighton Belle'

Opulence which the London Brighton & South Coast company bestowed on Brighton in 1875 with a Pullman service from London Victoria, was not matched by a totally enthusiastic response from affluent Victorian businessmen and tourists. This was partly because they objected to paying supplementary fares to travel in open saloons which robbed them of the privacy they enjoyed in compartment stock.

But as the LB&SC helped to promote Brighton as 'the Queen of Watering Places' and 'the premier holiday resort of England', the Pullmans became increasingly popular and a seven-car 'train de luxe', the first Pullman built in England, went into service in November 1908.

Four months earlier, the rebuilding of Victoria station had been completed and the main line had been widened to Three Bridges to cope with an increase in Brighton traffic.

The 'Southern Belle' of 1908 was an immediate success and ran until the early 1930s when the Southern Railway extended main line third-rail electrification and introduced the world's first all-electric Pullman service. It continued to carry its original name until being renamed 'Brighton Belle' some 18 months later.

By 1959, diesel multiple unit Pullmans were being built for services between London, Bristol, Manchester, Birmingham and Wolverhampton. The attractive streamlining of the sets gave them a modern profile very much in contrast to the stately home on wheels look of the Brighton units.

Strong public affection for the 'Brighton Belle' was reflected in protests when the Pullman livery was changed to a version of British Rail standard. And there was well-publicised discontent when kippers were taken off the menu. Unlike the livery, they soon returned.

The Pullmans just failed to reach their 40th birthday, being withdrawn in April 1972. Latter-day passengers sometimes had a rough ride. Peter Semmens noted in *Railway World*: 'Not only did our table rock alarmingly whenever anyone leant against it, but the windows "worked" and creaked in their frames like a wooden ship at sea.'

So the 15 'Brighton Belle' cars of 1933 were withdrawn by BR but all survive in a variety of uses; some working on preserved railways, some as restaurants.

Reading
Allen, C. J., *Titled Trains of Great Britain*
Gillham, J. C., *The Age of the Electric Train*

Below:
In 1969 the '5BEL' units were taken to Eastleigh Works where they were refurbished and appeared in the new blue and grey livery. Pictured at London Bridge, following diversion due to engineering work, on 19 April of that year, '5BEL' No 3052 demonstrates well the livery that the units wore for the last years of their operational career. The 'Brighton Belle' service was to be withdrawn three years later on 30 April 1972. *Chris Gammell*

Above right:
The down 'Brighton Belle' is caught at East Croydon on 26 July 1964 with '5BEL' No 3051 leading. The three Class 5BEL sets were the last Pullman units to be built for the Southern Railway, being constructed by Metropolitan-Cammell in 1932. Initially the new service for which the units were built was called the 'Southern Belle', but the name changed to the more familiar 'Brighton Belle' in 1934. *Chris Gammell*

Below right:
The interior of a second-class 'Brighton Belle' coach. *Colour-Rail*

A Visit to King's Cross Shed

'There is more to loco-spotting than merely noting numbers', Ian Allan wrote in the *Radio Times* in September 1959 as he publicised *Railway Roundabout* programmes then being transmitted on BBC1. 'There have been railway enthusiasts for many years but only during the last few years has loco-spotting developed into an organised hobby for younger enthusiasts.'

The IA Loco-spotters' club had over 370,000 members, some of whom went on to make a career in railways.

With modernisation well under way, Ian Allan wondered whether diesel and electric locomotives would become popular with loco-spotters, but added: 'I need not have worried as there is just as much excitement at seeing them as steam locomotives.'

Diesels as exciting as steam locomotives? Hardly, when young visitors lucky enough to get into King's Cross, or 'Top Shed' as it was known, could see Gresley Pacifics and other top-link locomotives. The cameras caught *Flying Scotsman* preparing to depart, tender piled high with coal, for a 4hr run to Leeds hauling the 'Yorkshire Pullman'.

'Top Shed' had a varied allocation ranging from express locomotives to powerful tanks working King's Cross suburban services. In 1959, the tanks were being gradually replaced by diesels. Early arrivals were North British Locomotive Type 2 Bo-Bo diesel-electrics, which had entered service only a few months earlier.

When it came to spotter-appeal, they were no match in beauty for the Gresley 'A4' Streamliners, or Class A1 Peppercorn Pacifics and Class V2 2-6-2 Green Arrows. The latter are still remembered as among the most graceful of mixed traffic designs.

The Streamliners worked the East Coast main line from King's Cross for years while the presence of the early diesels, except shunters, was short lived. The NBL Bo-Bos were in BR service for only 10 years and those originally allocated to the Eastern Region were later transferred to Scotland where they could be sent to the builder's works if they needed attention.

Reading
Cooper, B. K., *BR Motive Power Since 1948*
Also: Shed allocation books.

Below:
Class N2/4 No 69593 is seen at King's Cross shed on 14 October 1961. This was one of a number of the class delivered in 1928 and 1929 that were fitted with condensing equipment. This locomotive was built, as LNER No 2687, by the Yorkshire Engine Co. It became No 9593 in the LNER's 1946 renumbering scheme. *Colour-Rail*

Above right:
The old order is gradually replaced at 'Top Shed'. Alongside 'V2' 2-6-2 No 60906 and 'A4' Pacific No 60025 *Falcon* on 14 October 1961 is one of the Brush Type 2 diesel-electrics (later Class 31) that were being delivered in large numbers. *Colour-Rail*

Below right:
Two 'A1' Pacifics are seen alongside each other at King's Cross shed on 23 May 1958. On the left is No 60122 *Curlew* and on the right No 60139 *Sea Eagle*. At this time both locomotives were allocated to 34A, but both were transferred in April 1959 to Doncaster, No 60122 being withdrawn from there in November 1962 with No 60139 succumbing in June 1964 also from Doncaster. *Bruce Chapman Collection/Colour-Rail*

A Worcestershire Branch Line: The Birmingham & Gloucester Loop

When it realised the impact, publicity and educational value of the programmes, British Rail gave exceptional help to the team. To add interest — and glamour — to a portrait of the Birmingham & Gloucester Loop, a Midland Compound 4-4-0 was polished up and for two days, rostered to replace the usual large Fowler 2-6-4 tanks working local passenger trains between Birmingham New Street, Barnt Green, where the Loop began, and Ashchurch where the Birmingham and Bristol main line was regained.

The Loop was used by some freight trains to avoid the Lickey Incline, but the 33-mile line was never engineered to express standard by the Midland Railway which built it in the 1860s.

It ran through the Vale of Evesham, serving one of the richest and loveliest farming areas in England and staff at a string of wayside stations were kept busy, not so much with passengers, but handling fruit crops which had to be speedily distributed throughout the country.

There were junctions with three other lines of which two were rather remote branches. Alcester was the junction of a 6½-mile GWR single line to Bearley which closed to regular passenger trains a few days after the outbreak of World War 2. Broom Junction lay at the western end of the Stratford-upon-Avon & Midland Junction Railway.

At Evesham, the Loop had a station adjacent to the Oxford Worcester & Wolverhampton and a spur was built between them.

Loop passenger services changed little in pattern. In late Victorian years, the Midland ran four weekday trains each way taking about 1hr 30min between Barnt Green and Ashchurch. The route, which became LMS at Grouping, passed to the Western Region on Nationalisation, but there was little difference in timetables. Services were only a few minutes quicker than they had been 60 years earlier.

Redditch was the turn-back station for a number of local services from Birmingham New Street and today the five single miles between Barnt Green and Redditch form the western tip of the 25kV Birmingham Cross City line to Lichfield. EMUs run to a single platform at Redditch built a little north of the original station. The rest of the route closed years ago.

Reading
Davies, R. & Grant, M. D., *Forgotten Railways: Chilterns & Cotswolds*

Birmingham & Gloucester Loop

Barnt Green–Redditch
Distance: 5¼ miles
Owner: Midland Railway
Opened: 1859
Now part of Birmingham Cross City line

Redditch–Ashchurch
Distance: 28 miles
Opened: 1864–68
Closed: 17 June 1963 Redditch–Ashchurch for Passengers
1962–63 Alcester–Ashchurch for Goods
6 July 1964 Redditch–Alcester for Goods

Alcester-Bearley
Distance: 6½ miles
Owner: Great Western Railway
Opened: 1876
Closed: 25 September 1939 Regular for Passengers
1951 for Goods

Broom Junction–Stratford-upon-Avon Town
Distance: 8 miles
Owner: Stratford-upon-Avon & Midland Junction Railway
Opened: 1879
Closed: 16 June 1947 for Passengers
13 June 1960 for Goods

Above right:
Compound No 41157 awaits departure from Evesham on 11 November 1959. *Eric Russell/Colour-Rail*

Left:
Compound No 41157 is seen here at Wixford station. By the date of this train, Wixford station, which was situated between Broom and Alcester, had already been closed nine years, having lost its passenger services on 2 January 1950. *Eric Russell/Colour-Rail*

Saltley Shed 1959

The largest of the Birmingham area sheds, Saltley was popular with transport enthusiasts for years because they could travel by tram to a depot where steam was in profusion. Birmingham Corporation trams on routes 8 and 10 took about 15min to reach Duddeston Mill Road from the city centre.

In summer 1945, I tried — and failed — to get into Saltley shed through the main entrance, but I enjoyed spotting LMS Garratt 2-6-6-2s working long coal trains into Washwood Heath yard, as they continued to do until the early 1950s.

(A more attractive place where I watched Garratts, the largest locomotives to run in Britain, was from the hills of the Derbyshire Peak District overlooking Gowhole Sidings, near Chinley.)

The first shed at Saltley, a round house, was completed by the Midland Railway in 1856, but quickly became overcrowded. It was replaced by larger ones opened in 1868 and 1876 on the opposite side of the Birmingham–Derby main line.

Classic Midland 0-6-0s of LMS Classes 3F and 4F were prominent among Saltley's 170 locomotives in 1959. But their days were numbered as steam gave way to diesel traction and, during the next few years, the shed allocation was reduced by about two-thirds leaving only BR standard classes. They were mainly of '5MT' 4-6-0s and '9F' 2-10-0s.

The 2-10-0s worked long distances including overnight fast freights via Derby and Sheffield to Carlisle. A more local diagram was the replacement of Lickey bankers when Bromsgrove (21C) was short of them.

Saltley has been solely a Locomotive Servicing Depot since closure to steam on completion of 25kV electrification in the Birmingham area in 1967.

The 'B' shed in the 21 group was Bournville, which was also Midland-built. Among its 30 locomotives in 1959 were four Midland Compound 4-4-0s working local passenger services.

Bournville closed in 1960 and was demolished, but part of a perimeter wall survived 'to echo to the sound of Cross-City line services as they pass by' as Paul Collins noted in *Britain's Rail Super Centres Birmingham*.

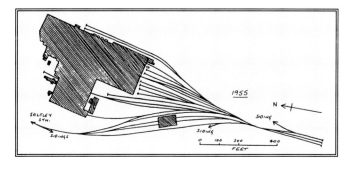

Western Region '45xx' Tanks

The 1959 video opened in winter gloom and sadness with the closure of the Wye Valley branches. It ends with a return visit to the Brent–Kingsbridge (for Salcombe) line in South Devon which survived a few more years.

The Kingsbridge branch was first seen in 1958 when camping coaches at Gara Bridge were featured. The 1959 visit was for a portrait of GWR '45xx' tanks, among the smallest of British Prairie tank designs, which accounts possibly for several of them having been preserved. When I rode No 4588 from Paignton to Kingswear while compiling a programme for Radio 4, the cab was cosy although a gale was roaring in from the English Channel.

The commentary explained the differences between two versions of the class. Engines of the original 1906 series had flat top side tanks with a 1,000gal capacity while the second series had tanks carrying another 300gal giving them a more useful range.

Such statistics contradicted the company's own publication *GWR Engines, Names, Numbers, Types, Classes etc*. It showed both designs — Nos 4500–4599 and 5500–5574 — as having the higher water capacity.

The Kingsbridge branch served large areas of South Devon and even in the climate of change in the late 1950s, its future was considered secure. Reviewing the branch in *Trains Illustrated* in February 1958, R. C. Sambourne noted: 'It is extremely unlikely that this line, with its incessant stream of holiday traffic during the summer months and its all-the-year-round freight traffic, will be closed, since it can hardly be a financial burden or an uneconomic proposition. One therefore visualizes immaculate diesel railcars running sedately through the peaceful and friendly Avon Valley before very long.'

But no railcars arrived, even after the closure in September 1961 of the single-track engine shed at Kingsbridge, home of a '45xx' tank, or an occasional 0-6-0 pannier tank, sub-shedded from Newton Abbot.

Two years later, the branch closed completely. A group of enthusiasts attempted to preserve it, but BR lifted the track before agreement could be negotiated.

Instead, the Dart Valley line was saved and so today enthusiasts recall holiday journeys over a host of short South Devon branches, by travelling north from the South Devon main line at Totnes rather than south from Brent to Kingsbridge.

Reading
See 'Camping Coaches'.

Below:
Looking pristine in its green livery, '4575' class 2-6-2T No 4587 glistens in the sun at Brent in June 1958. The '4575' series of Prairie tanks were introduced in 1927 to a design by Collett. At this time No 4587 was allocated to Truro, from where it was withdrawn in August 1960.
P. J. Hughes/Colour-Rail (BRW1269)

Above right:
No 4591 shunts alongside Launceston's substantial shed in December 1962. Then allocated to Laira, No 4591 was to pass to Yeovil in May 1963 before transferring finally to Swindon in July 1964, from where it was withdrawn the same month. *Peter Gray/Colour-Rail (BRW914)*

Below right:
A work-stained '45xx' 2-6-2T No 4588 departs from Yelverton with the 10.15 service from Launceston to Plymouth on a beautiful early spring day in February 1962. *Peter Gray/Colour-Rail (BRW913)*

Left:
'45xx' 2-6-2T No 4574 backs the Kingsbridge freight into the substantial goods shed at Brent in August 1962. The Kingsbridge branch, which opened in December 1893 was to last for almost 70 years before complete closure came on 16 September 1963.
Rob Tibbits/Colour-Rail (BRW1133)

Below:
'45xx' 2-6-2T No 4570 slides into Shaugh Bridge Platform with a local service from Tavistock to Plymouth via Yelverton in June 1962. The station at Shaugh Bridge opened on 21 August 1907 and closed, along with the rest of the route, to passenger services on 31 December 1962.
C. Trethewey/Colour-Rail (BRW1081)

Thornaby Motive Power Depot

As a major depot for lumbering goods engines, Thornaby shed lacked the glamour of King's Cross shed, yet it found a place in history as an unusual project carried out as part of the 1955 Modernisation plan. It was designed to meet the transition from the dying age of steam to that of modern traction.

Major modernisation of local railways included 'marrying' of old goods yards into Teeside Marshalling Yard with 66 miles of track and 153 sidings. The Darlington–Saltburn line, which bisected the sites, was diverted for almost a mile to run south of yard and shed.

When Thornaby shed was filmed, the marshalling yard was still in the future, not being opened until September 1963.

The shed, covering 70 acres, replaced Newport (51B), Middlesbrough (51D), Stockton (51E) and Haverton Hill (51G). Built to service 220 steam locomotives, it was dominated by a coaling tower storing up to 350 tons and able to coal four locomotives simultaneously. Among the first allocation were veteran 0-8-0s, a type developed by the North Eastern Railway to handle a variety of heavy mineral trains. The film featured BR No 63364, formerly LNER Class Q6.

They were very much on home ground, the class of more than 100 having been designed by Raven and built by the North Eastern Railway at Darlington between 1913 and 1921.

More than a third of the locomotives could be housed under cover in adjacent straight-road and octagonal sheds. The latter incorporated long girders salvaged during modernisation of Bradford Forster Square passenger station.

The octagonal shed features in all five *Railway Roundabout* videos with a pan shot of locomotives with tenders facing the turntable, forming a striking back-cloth to the production credits of each video.

Today, Thornaby is the depot of a number of heavy diesel freight locomotives of Classes 56 and 60, which work long-distance diagrams, and Class 08 and 09 diesel shunters.

Occasionally, steam returns. It was at Thornaby that Class A2 4-6-2 No 60532 *Blue Peter* was repaired after the wheelslip which destroyed its valve gear in 1994.

Reading
Unattributed, *Railway Magazine*, 'New Motive Power Depot at Thornaby, North Eastern Region', October 1958.
Unattributed, *Rail* magazine 276 of 1996 gives a depot profile, 'Tees Marshalling Yard, North Eastern Region, BR'.

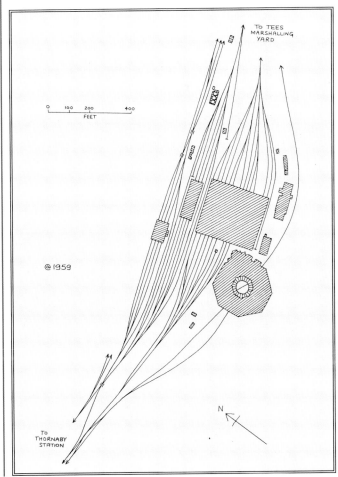

Typical of many Scottish Region trains at this period is this Stanier Class 5-hauled train pictured at Stirling on 9 July 1965. No 45084 is seen at the head of a local train for Glasgow. *Neil Caplan*

1960

A Visit to Perth Shed

Viewing the variety of locomotives, steam and diesel, filmed on Perth shed and trying to write down their numbers without stopping the video, reminded me of spotting days! How frenetic it used to be leaning out of windows and scribbling numbers in notebooks.

Perth shed of BR days was on the down side of the Glasgow main line south of the station. Long and heavy trains bound for the Highland and Dundee and Aberdeen lines would have been travelling more slowly than today's Class 158 units which run past a food supermarket built on part of its site at Friarton.

Until Grouping, Perth was the meeting place of three major companies: the Caledonian, Highland and North British. Their individuality, gently eroded after Grouping, further ebbed away under LMS and LNER regimes. Yet it was still evident a decade after Nationalisation.

After Grouping, the London Midland & Scottish Railway closed the former Highland Railway shed at Perth and the former 'Caley' shed was improved.

Locomotives on shed in 1960 formed as diverse and fascinating a variety as any which could still be found in

Britain by the 1960s. There were classes with shapely round splashers and straight running-boards and cylinders inside and out: none escaped the commentator's eye.

For years from 1930 Perth was the northern terminus of a 296-mile Crewe North (5A) men and engine link, which Allan Baker and Gavin Morrison described in *Crewe Sheds* as among the toughest footplate diagrams ever regularly assigned in Britain: 'Perth men, it should be noted, never came to Crewe, or south of Carlisle for that matter!'

Far from dying as the 1955 Modernisation programme gathered momentum, Scottish steam enjoyed an Indian summer. Two years after the *Railway Roundabout* visit, Gresley 'A4s' spearheaded a 3hr Glasgow–Aberdeen express service with four intermediate stops including Perth, where several minutes were allowed for taking water on the platform.

Lightweight corridor formations were well within the capabilities of the 'A4s', then beginning to come to the end of their lives.

The Glasgow–Aberdeen steam link ended in autumn 1966 and a year later the Caledonian main line from Stanley Junction, north of Perth, to Kinnaber Junction, was closed and expresses diverted via Dundee.

While that economy robbed Perth of another of its services, it benefited subsequently from the restoration of passenger services over the scenically-attractive former North British branch from Ladybank. This is now the quickest route between Perth and Edinburgh, although a more intensive service is maintained via Stirling.

Reading
Robin, G. H., *Trains Illustrated* February 1957, 'Resorts for Railfans: Perth'

Below:
Ex-Caledonian Railway 4-4-0 No 54485 is seen under the coaling stage at Perth shed on 19 May 1960. Designed by Pickersgill and built at St Rollox, No 54485 was built in September 1920 and originally numbered 80 by the Caledonian. It became No 14485 at the Grouping in 1923 and was withdrawn in October 1961. *Eric Russell/Colour-Rail*

On the Spey River Line

Today's railway passenger services map of North East Scotland consists of a huge circle embracing Perth, Dundee, Aberdeen and Inverness. It resembles a buckled bicycle wheel which has collapsed because all its spokes have been thrown away.

Inside the rim there is one fragment, the southern five miles, as far as the Boat of Garten, of the original Highland main line between Aviemore and Inverness via Forres. It forms the enthusiast-preserved Strathspey Railway which plans to reopen part of the Speyside line. This was completed by the Great North of Scotland Railway from Boat of Garten to its Elgin–Keith line at Craigellachie on 3 August 1866.

The GNS was the smallest of the five independent Scottish railways yet it was the only one with 'Great' in its title. After Grouping, it became a remote part of the London & North Eastern Railway.

The Spey River line ran through sparsely populated countryside and the only sizeable town, Grantown-on-Spey, was better served by the Highland main line on which it was the last stop for Forres-bound trains before they climbed north to Dava summit.

The Highland and Speyside lines, both single, ran side by side for a short distance as they left Boat of Garten.

In 1960, Highland and GNS trains between Boat of Garten and Grantown (West and East) were both allowed 17min for the nine miles. When both routes closed in autumn 1965, Scotland lost over 60 miles of passenger railways: 31 miles between Boat of Garten and Forres and the 33½ miles of the Speyside line.

The remoteness of the Speyside route could be detected by timetable sleuths who may have found a footnote in *Bradshaw's* stating that Ballindalloch was the station for Tomintoul '15 miles distant'. I have yet to discover whether *Bradshaw's* named any other town or village as far distant from its 'local' station.

Another subject perhaps worthy of study on a winter's night is how many halts in Britain were named after farms or cottages? There were three among four halts in the 14 intermediate stops on the Speyside line.

By 1960, steam was being displaced by diesel railbuses, the flexibility of the new traction being exploited by the introduction in November 1958 of a railbus service between Aviemore and Elgin. The 51-mile journeys, which took nearly two hours, continued until 1965. After the railbus service was withdrawn, freight trains continued to use the Strathspey route until November 1968.

Reading
Vallance, H. A., *The Great North of Scotland Railway*

Strathspey Railway
Distance: 33½ miles
Owner: Great North of Scotland Railway
Boat of Garten–Craigellachie
Opened: 1863–1866
Closed: 18 October 1965 completely

Aviemore–Boat of Garten-Forres
Distance: 36 miles
Owner: Highland Railway
Opened: 3 August 1863
Closed: 18 October 1965 for Passengers
Boat of Garten–Forres for Goods
4 November 1968 Aviemore–Boat of Garten
for Goods
Reopened: Summer 1978 Aviemore–Boat of Garten as the
Strathspey Railway

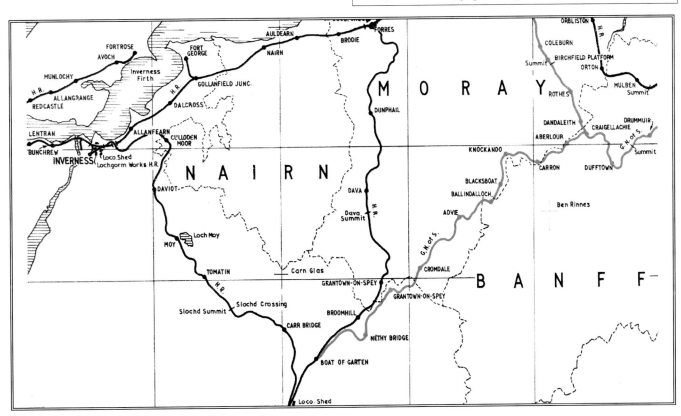

Adams Tanks on the Lyme Regis Line

Of the many railway attractions which an enthusiast could enjoy during summer holidays in the West Country, the Lyme Regis branch was among the most fascinating. It was the most easterly of a group which ran to seaside resorts from the London & South Western West of England main line between Salisbury and Exeter.

Lyme Regis is in Dorset but has the flavour of East Devon, the county of the other towns: Seaton, Sidmouth, Budleigh Salterton and Exmouth. Today only Exmouth can be reached by rail over a single line running beside the Exe estuary from Exeter.

The Axminster–Lyme Regis line of almost seven miles had the strongest appeal because it was worked by a trio of Adams 4-4-2 radial tanks.

Usually they were in charge of a single-corridor coach but in summer some Saturday expresses included a Lyme Regis portion which had to be double-headed by the tanks over the branch to the resort 151 rail-miles from the capital.

Branch journeys took about 20min, punctuated by a single stop at Combpyne, which had the only passing loop until the Southern Railway converted it into a siding in 1930.

Railways came late to Lyme Regis. A branch was first mooted among three schemes born of the 1845 Railway Mania, but it was not until the passing of the Light Railway Act of 1896 that the final impetus came from a local company which got an LRO in 1899. Two years later, Baedeker guides were still advising travellers that: 'From Axminster a coach runs several times daily (railway under construction) to Lyme Regis, a picturesquely-situated seaport and bathing place (2,095 inhabitants).' It was not until late in the summer season of 1903 that the first holidaymakers arrived by rail. Trains were worked by the L&SWR which absorbed the local company in 1907.

Summer Saturdays were the only days on which the line was busy. *Bradshaw's* winter 1960 timetable showed buses replacing trains on the first service from Lyme Regis to Axminster at 6.31am, and the last evening return. Southern National Omnibus services ran between Langford's shop at Axminster and Lyme Regis Post Office, rather than the railway stations. Buses took 27min — 6min longer than the trains.

This was a period of change, heralded by *Trains Illustrated Summer Annual* No 4 carrying an ominous warning: 'As we go to press, the signs of permanent way work provoke the suspicion that the trio of tanks may soon be replaced by more modern power.' And from July 1961, Ivatt 2-6-2 tanks worked the goods service until it was withdrawn in winter 1964 and the passenger service which survived until November 1965 when the branch closed completely.

Reading
Somerville, C., *Walking Old Railways*

Axminster–Lyme Regis	
Distance:	6¾ miles
Owner:	London & South Western Railway
Opened:	24 August 1903
Closed:	3 February 1964 for Goods
	29 November 1965 for Passengers

Below:
Radial Tank No 30584 is seen at the branch terminus of Lyme Regis on 15 March 1960. *Colour-Rail*

Above right:
Two of the surviving Radial Tanks, Nos 30584 and 30582, are caught double-heading at Combpyne. By this date only three of the 1882-designed Adams 4-4-2Ts remained in service. *J. G. Dewing/Colour-Rail*

Below right:
The Lyme Regis branch met the London & South Western main line from Waterloo to Exeter at Axminster. Here, one of the surviving trio, No 30582, awaits its next duty. A total of 71 of Adams 'O415' class were built between 1882 and 1885. All were withdrawn in the 1920s with the exception of two retained for the Lyme Regis branch; these were supplemented by a third reacquired by the Southern Railway from the independent East Kent Railway in 1946. Only one of the class, ex-No 30583, survives and can today be seen on the Bluebell Railway. *P. B. Whitehouse/Colour-Rail*

'T9s' to Tavistock

As the beginning of the commentary reminds viewers, 1960 was the Indian summer of many of the ancient locomotives of the Southern Region. It was also that of the group of ex-Southern Region lines west of Exeter which have gone down in history nicknamed the 'Withered Arm'. Their backbone was the former London & South Western main line to Plymouth.

With trains worked by locomotives like 'T9' 4-4-0s, the lines retained their character, individuality and charm which made them so totally different from those of the GWR, including the route of the 'Cornish Riviera', which broadly served the same area of the West Country.

Okehampton was the hub of the 'Withered Arm', a station where the 'Atlantic Coast Express' from Waterloo to Plymouth was booked to stop for 20min to detach coaches for Bude (31 miles) and Padstow (62 miles).

It was not timings or distances that attracted enthusiasts, but the chance to see Drummond's 'T9' 4-4-0s — Greyhounds by looks and deeds. The few survivors of an LSWR class of 66 were, by 1960, the oldest express passenger engines still in service, although their duties were semi-fast.

They ran over lines which took their character from 'the granite and high tors and deep combes of Dartmoor', to quote an attractive Southern Railway pocket guide of the 1930s, *Let's Get Out Here*. It listed 26 walks on the route of the 'ACE' including one which took ramblers under the 150ft-high lattice Meldon viaduct, near Okehampton.

Economies took place over several years. After 1963 boundary changes, the Western Region downgraded the Plymouth route and closed it completely between Okehampton and Bere Alston in May 1968. Okehampton–Exeter passenger services continued until summer 1972. The line still serves Meldon quarry, bought from BR in 1994 by a private company. It has restored Meldon viaduct, a scheduled ancient monument. From Crediton, the quarry access line runs beside the Barnstaple branch to the former Yeoford Junction.

Wadebridge–Halwill Junction and the Padstow branches lost their passenger services in October 1966, and Devon lost another long branch — one not associated with the 'Withered Arm' — on the same day. It was the 45-mile ex-GWR secondary route between Barnstaple and Taunton. Western Region timetables showed connections over the steeply graded Barnstaple–Ilfracombe branch, which was to survive until October 1970.

Bude continued to have a passenger service via Wadebridge to the GWR main line at Bodmin Road until January 1967. Part of Wadebridge station has been converted into the John Betjeman Centre commemorating the poet who loved Cornwall and railways.

The Exeter–Barnstaple branch survives. And in the best traditions of GWR and SR publicity departments which worked so hard to attract tourists to Devon, it is picturesquely named the 'Tarka Line' in current passenger timetables.

The line is characteristic of the LSWR west of Exeter in the sense that like the Bude and Padstow branches, it is lengthy, Barnstaple being 38 miles from Exeter St Davids.

Reading
Atterbury, P., *AA Discovering Britain's Lost Railways*

Below:
Pictured at Bere Alston in 1960, No 30729 was Dubs & Co-built Works No 3772 in January 1900. The locomotive was to have an operational life of more than 60 years, being withdrawn from Exmouth Junction shed in March 1961. *Harry Luff*

Above right:
'T9' 4-4-0 No 30338 is pictured at Okehampton on 19 April 1960 with a down service for Bude. No 30338 (as London & South Western No 338) was the last of the 'T9s' to be built at Nine Elms Works (in October 1901) and was also the penultimate of the class to be completed. The locomotive was withdrawn in April 1961 from Exmouth Junction shed and was one of the last of the type to remain in service. *Colour-Rail*

Below right:
Constructed by Dubs & Co (Works No 3759) in July 1899, 'T9' No 30715 is seen at Egloskerry on 19 April 1960 with an up service from Padstow. No 30715 was to remain in service until July 1961, being outlasted only by the preserved No 30120 which succumbed two years later. *Colour-Rail*

Devon/Cornwall: Selective Closure Dates: London & South Western Railway Main Line and Branches

Exeter–Plymouth Main Line

Okehampton–Bere Alston
Distance: 20 miles
Closed: 28 February 1966 for Goods
6 May 1968 for Passengers
(Plymouth–Bere Alston [10 miles]–
Gunnislake [15 miles] still open.)

Okehampton–Exeter
Distance: 25 miles
Closed: 5 June 1972 for Passengers

Bude Branch

Okehampton–Halwill Junction (12½ miles)–Bude
Distance: 31 miles
Closed: 3 October 1966 for Passengers

Padstow Branch

Okehampton–Wadebridge–Padstow
Distance: 62 miles
Closed: 3 October 1966 for Passengers

Padstow–Bodmin Road
Distance: 16½ miles
Closed: LSWR/GWR 30 January 1967 for Passengers

Two 'Dukedogs' to Barmouth

Watching double-headed 'Dukedogs' against a Cambrian back-cloth put me in philosophical mood, possibly because I knew Cambrian steam for many years. I reflected that one of the delights of railways which an enthusiast quickly learns is that they can be found in infinite variety.

After more than half a century of studying and writing about them, I feel I know little and still enjoy the satisfaction of learning something new.

This happened when the Talyllyn Railway Preservation Society special, which was the 'Dukedogs' charge, paused at Cemmes Road, in the Upper Dovey valley five miles east of Machynlleth. The commentator revealed that it was common practice for the old companies to add the suffix 'road' to stations some distance from the town or village they served.

While stopped at Cemmes Road, the locomotive crews talked with the then Divisional Superintendent at Shrewsbury, Oliver Veltom, who saved the Vale of Rheidol narrow gauge line from closure in BR days and helped preservationists in mid-Wales in many ways.

I knew him as a senior officer conscious of the social value of railways in lightly populated areas like mid-Wales. He was deeply saddened by economies and when I visited his home overlooking the Llanfyllin branch, he told me he drew the curtains as the last trains passed in January 1965.

Pat Whitehouse must have taken pride in the running of the special for he was a founder member of the Talyllyn Preservation Society. On reaching Towyn (as it was spelt in 1960), members transferred to a narrow gauge special hauled by locomotive No 4 *Edward Thomas*, fitted with a Geisl Ejector. The commentator maintained that had ruined its appearance. But it seems it was welcome, for Norman Harvey reported in the *Stephenson Locomotive Society Journal* in August 1961 that he had heard 'most encouraging reports of its success' from a Talyllyn driver.

Unlike footplate crews, passengers on specials run through mid-Wales in the dying years of steam enjoyed comforts and facilities that were not usually found on scheduled services. The 1960 Talyllyn special was no exception, carrying sleeping cars because of a late night departure from Towyn.

In December 1962, local people stood on snowy platforms and in farmhouse doorways to wave farewell to an SLS Sunday special which formed the last train from Moat Lane to Brecon and from there to Hereford.

Its passengers could buy refreshments — something never available to those travelling on branch trains.

Reading

Christiansen, Rex and Miller, R. W., *The Cambrian Railways Volumes 1 and 2*.
Trains Illustrated Summer Annual, 1960

Below:
Caught in the sun, 'Dukedogs'; Nos 9004 and 9017 make a superb picture as caught by the camera of Eric Russell at Llwyngwril in 1960. No 9004 by this date had lost its allocated name (*Earl of Dartmouth*), whilst No 9017, although allocated the name *Earl of Berkeley*, remained anonymous during its career with both the Great Western and British Railways. By the date of this photograph both of the locomotives were coming to the end of their career; No 9004 was withdrawn in June 1960 and No 9017 four months later. Fortunately, No 9017 was to be preserved and today can be seen on the Bluebell Railway restored as GWR No 3217. *Eric Russell/Colour-Rail*

Above right:
Taken at Towyn (as the town's name was then spelt), Nos 9004 (again) and 9014 are seen at the head of a Talyllyn Railway special — notice the headboard (and the evidence of a trackside fire!) — on 26 April 1959. No 9014 was allocated (but never carried) the name *Earl Waldegrave*; it was withdrawn in October 1960. *W. P. de Beer/Colour-Rail*

Below right:
It is a frightening fact that No 3217 has now been preserved for more than 35 years, a period longer than it was operated by either the Great Western Railway or British Railways. This photograph of the 'Dukedog' illustrates the point well; it was taken in its 'as withdrawn' condition at Sheffield Park on 1 April 1962, more than 30 years ago. *R. C. Riley*

Two Caley Bogies from Perth to Aviemore

The diesel-hauled 'Royal Highlander', the HSTs and Class 158s which grace the Highland line today are actors on an old stage. For the setting of the line and the line itself have changed little through the years.

When the doors of a Class 158 spring open and enthusiasts step on to a wayside platform somewhere north of Perth and look towards the hills, they may still feel a sense of detachment from the workaday world.

The 83-mile journey to Aviemore is full of atmosphere, established by double-headed false starts made out of Perth station. As railway programmes became more popular on television, BR operators got increasing requests for them. I made one during filming in colour for BBC Television archives of the last days of steam in North West England.

It took place before colour television was fully introduced in Britain. The train BR controllers selected after discussions was a morning Euston–Blackpool South express, 'Black 5' hauled from Preston. It was an inspired choice for on that occasion the express had loaded to nine, rather than six bogies.

False starts made at intermediate stations produced magnificent close-up shots of slowly turning wheels and hissing steam: as memorable as the Perth starts eight years earlier.

'Black 5s' first reached the Highlands in summer 1934 and by the early 1950s more than 70 were allocated to Perth shed. They were often piloted by Caley bogies on heavy expresses, including those between Glasgow and Inverness.

One was routed over the original Highland Railway line from Aviemore to Inverness via Dava summit rather than the direct line via Slochd. The 26-mile direct line revolutionised the Highland rail network when it opened in 1898. The next major change to the network came with closure of the Dava route between Aviemore and Forres in October 1965.

Today, trains not booked to stop at three of the eight intermediate stations cover the 118 miles from Perth to Inverness in 2 hours 10 minutes. That is less than half the time taken by some Highland Railway services making up to 20 station stops.

For years, there was a fascinating variety of passenger services over the Highland main line. The LNWR regarded them as important enough to include them in its own passenger timetables.

Reading
Vallance, H. A., *The Highland Railway*

Below:
A dramatic view from the footplate of No 54486 — one of the two Caledonian 4-4-0s used for the run north to Inverness — sees Nos 54485 and 54486 heading towards Dalnaspidal on the climb towards Druimuachdar Summit on the 6.5pm service on 20 May 1960.
Eric Russell/Colour-Rail

Above right:
On the following day (21 May 1960) the two ex-Caledonian Railway veterans headed south from Inverness over the original Highland Railway main line via Grantown-on-Spey to Aviemore as the 2.5pm service from Inverness. The train is seen here at Forres. No 54486 was the last of the batch of 4-4-0s built at St Rollox in 1920; it was to outlast No 54485 by a few months, being withdrawn in March 1962.
Eric Russell/Colour-Rail

Below right:
With No 54485 leading No 54486, the pair head along the now abandoned section of the former Highland main line at Dunphail Viaduct. The ex-HR main line from Aviemore to Forres was closed in 1965, but the Strathspey Railway preserved the section from Aviemore to Boat of Garten and is now slowly rebuilding north of Boat of Garten to Grantown-on-Spey. *Eric Russell/Colour-Rail*

Trains at Newcastle upon Tyne

Throughout railway history few greater contrasts could be found than those between a remote country junction like Boat of Garten and a large main line complex as big as Newcastle upon Tyne.

The change of mood and atmosphere was caught well by the cameras, the Newcastle scene being introduced by a shunter: ex-LNER Class J72 0-6-0 tank No 68723 carrying both the former North Eastern Railway and BR crests.

The commentary tells much of the unusual history of the class which earned a place in *The Historic Locomotive Pocketbook* by H. C. Casserley. He noted: 'This remarkable little design stands unique in being constructed over a period of 53 years, under three different stages of railway ownership and five regimes of locomotive superintendent.'

Contrast, too, in motive power: between the 'J72' and an English Electric 1Co-Co1 D264, later to be renumbered into Class 40 — the first class of diesel-electric locomotives for main line passenger work to enter service under the BR Modernisation Plan.

The first was built in 1958, only eight years after the last of the last batch of 'J72s'.

More prominent at Newcastle were the EE predecessors — Gresley non-streamlined 'Pacifics'. In 1960, they were far from being displaced as I found the following year when I was on the footplate of Class A1 No 60148 *Aboyeur* from York to Newcastle with the 'Heart of Midlothian' express on a misty autumn afternoon.

At Newcastle, one of the most famous Class A3s — No 60096 *Papyrus* — newly out-shopped, waited to hook on. So began another memorable footplate run with speeds well into the 80s through Northumberland.

Part of the fascination of railways in steam days was in spotting different classes of locomotives working crack expresses. In the mid-1950s, Peppercorn Class A1 Pacifics were almost invariably in charge of the 'Queen of Scots' all-Pullman expresses.

In 1960, 'A3' No 60036 *Colombo* is seen departing from Newcastle with the Up 'Queen of Scots'. The express had left Edinburgh 2hr 25min earlier for the run south to Leeds via Harrogate and King's Cross, which it was not due to reach for another 6hr.

Its route from the East Coast main line at Northallerton through Ripon to Harrogate (Dragon Junction) was later to become a casualty of modernisation, being closed in March 1967.

Newcastle's magnificent station has changed in recent years but without loss of character. It has swopped third-rail suburban electrification for that of the Tyne & Wear Metro, completed 1980-84, which runs under the station, and, of course, the East Coast main line electrification. No 1 platform is now the only one of those in the main station once used by the LNER two-car articulated units introduced on the North Tyneside lines in 1937–38.

Reading
Gillham, J. C., *The Age of the Electric Train*

Below:
Pictured at Newcastle in 1961, 'J72' No 68723 had been repainted into North Eastern Railway livery for use as station pilot. The 'J72s' were probably unique in British railway history, in being constructed over a 63-year period by three different railways — the North Eastern built 75 between 1898 and 1921, the LNER 10 in 1925 and BR an additional 29 between 1949 and 1951! *Colour-Rail*

Above right:
With the trainshed of Newcastle Central as a backdrop, 'A3' Pacific No 60084 *Trigo* — one of the class fitted with a double blast pipe and chimney — awaits departure with the southbound 'Queen of Scots' Pullman service on 12 September 1960. At this time No 60084 was allocated to Leeds Neville Hill shed; it was transferred to Gateshead in December 1963 from where it was withdrawn in November 1964. *George M. Staddon/Colour-Rail*

Below right:
A 1920-built South Tyne electric unit, headed by No E29187, enters High Shields station in September 1954. *C. Woodhead/Colour-Rail (DE1611)*

Trains at York

Steam was also in abundance at York, where the East Coast route theme was further captured by the cameras. Gresley and Thompson Pacifics were again the stars, notably the streamlined A4s running through with the 'Flying Scotsman' and the 'Elizabethan', which also ran non-stop over the 393 miles between King's Cross and Edinburgh. When its schedule was cut to 6¼hr in 1964, it became a mile-a-minute express.

'From then on,' wrote Cecil J. Allen in *Titled Trains of Great Britain*, 'the working of the "Elizabethan", with a gross load of about 420 to 425 tons, became one of the most exciting duties ever required of a steam locomotive in Great Britain; it was entrusted, of course, to a Gresley A4 Pacific.'

One of the original Class J72 tanks, No 68677, is seen working as station pilot before a visit is paid to York's original Railway Museum. It is often forgotten that this was Britain's first Railway Museum, founded by officials of the North Eastern Railway in 1922, just before that company lost its identity at Grouping, and opened by the LNER in 1928.

Small exhibits were displayed in what was once the refreshment room of York's second station just inside the city's historic walls. It was used by passengers from 1841 until the present universally admired station opened in 1877.

The large-exhibits section of the museum with its collection of historic locomotives, was housed in locomotive and carriage workshops close by.

The museum itself seemed time-warped, being run in a style unimaginable in today's necessary atmosphere of high security. A 1953 leaflet explained to visitors: 'There is no charge and there are no formalities. There is no array of uniformed attendants, but there is always someone there who "knows all the answers" if asked questions.'

I often chatted to 'that someone' as he worked at a desk hidden behind a full length curtain, draped theatre-style in a corner of the building.

The museum did not have a viewing area like the National establishment opened in 1975. Spotters simply walked out of the old buildings and went to the station platforms.

In 1960 York was a junction where steam seemed far from extinction. There was just a hint of it on film: the sight of early BR DMUs on a service to Scarborough. Proof that the resort's freight was still steam-hauled, was provided by a Class K1 2-6-0 Mogul departing for the seaside.

The North Eastern Railway placed York at the centre of its 'octopus-like' system with lines radiating in all directions. Today, as historian Peter Semmens pointed out in the *Railway Magazine* in March 1996, almost twice as many trains use the station now as they did soon after Nationalisation.

Reading

Appleby, K., *Britain's Rail Super Centres: York*, Ian Allan Publishing

Adams, John & Whitehouse, Pat, *Railway Roundabout: The Book of the TV Programme*

Hunter Davies, *A Walk Along The Tracks*

Rolt, L. T. C., *The Railway Museum, York*

Below:
Class A4 Pacific No 60034 *Lord Faringdon* is seen at York with a southbound service on 17 April 1957. One of the King's Cross (Top Shed) allocated members of the class, No 60034 was, like other examples, transferred to Scottish Region once their top-link duties on the East Coast main line ceased. In No 60034's case transfer came in October 1963 when, after four months at Neasden, it migrated northwards to Aberdeen. It was withdrawn in August 1966. *The late W. Oliver/Colour-Rail*

Above right:
One of the more unusual exhibits in the old Railway Museum in York was the ex-North Eastern Railway 2-2-4T No 66 *Aerolite* seen here on 20 April 1954. Classified 'X1' by the LNER, No 66 had a long and involved history. First constructed as a 2-2-2WT in 1851, it was rebuilt as a 2-2-2T in 1886 and again as a 4-4-2T in 1892. Finally, in 1902, it appeared as a 2-2-4T compound!. Withdrawn finally in 1934, it was preserved and can now be seen at the National Railway Museum. *Eric Russell/Colour-Rail*

Below right:
Class A3 No 60056 *Centenary* blows off at York as it awaits departure with a northbound service on 29 August 1959. Constructed at Doncaster in February 1925 (as LNER No 2555), the locomotive gained its name through the fact that 1925 was the centenary of the opening of the Stockton & Darlington Railway. At this date the locomotive was allocated to Grantham, from where it was withdrawn in May 1963. *Eric Russell/Colour-Rail*

The Cromford & High Peak Railway

I realised the hell early railway passengers must have suffered riding in open coaches when a railtour over the Cromford & High Peak Railway ran into a thunderstorm.

The deluge, which occurred on one of the highest and most exposed sections, also soaked dozens of members of the Stephenson Locomotive Society (North West area) and the Manchester Locomotive Society. For several hours, there was nowhere to get dry or to change clothes.

In fireside comfort, sit back and enjoy this film as one of pure delight, full of the atmosphere of this unusual railway which ran 'over the hills and far away'. This colour film, shot in sunshine, is perhaps the most fascinating and important screened on *Railway Roundabout* because film cameras were able to capture more vividly than any other type, the character of one of Britain's earliest railways.

To the end, it had a strong Victorian atmosphere, partly because so much of its machinery and operating methods dated from that era. It was still a spectacular railway long after similarly worked standard gauge incline railways had been closed.

Built to connect two canals, the line climbed nearly 1,000ft from the Midland Railway Derby–Manchester main line at High Peak Junction, to Parsley Hay on the Buxton–Ashbourne route via two long and steep rope-worked inclines. The Victorian travel writer M. J. B. Baddeley noted in 1894 that its course was 'unequalled in Britain for abrupt curves and breakneck gradients'.

It survived years longer than many branches because, besides handling stone traffic, it took water to quarries, factories and cottages. It was carried in two converted LNWR tenders — almost as interesting as the locomotives which the company allocated to the line. Among these were Webb 2-4-0 'Chopper' tanks, which ran only on the level between Sheep Pasture and Middleton inclines. Forever associated with the line were ex-North London Railway 0-6-0 tanks, the last of which, seen at work, is now preserved.

In the years before closure, the C&HP became a magnet for enthusiasts and a number of tours, steam-hauled as far as possible, were run. Part of the route of one I joined in April 1961 was from Buxton to Edale on the Hope Valley line between Chinley and Sheffield. It was then under closure threat, but was reprieved and today is the main artery between North West England, South Yorkshire and the East Midlands.

After closure, the C&HP took on a new role as a walking trail with its own 'junction' to the Tissington Trail, created from much of the far more level Buxton–Ashbourne route.

Tourists were offered free walk-sheets stored in weather-proof boxes in car parks. They showed the trails and their setting in limestone hills, little changed from the days when the Peak District was full of interesting railways, including the Manchester Central–Derby main line with expresses that gave magnificent views from carriage windows, even on the wettest of days.

Reading
Lovett Jones, G., *Railway Walks: Exploring Disused Railways*
Vinter, Jeff., *Railway Walks: LMS*

Cromford Canal Wharf–Hurdlow
Distance: 15½ miles
Owner: The Cromford & High Peak Railway
Operator: London & North Western Railway (leased from 1861; vested 1887)
Opened: 29 May 1830
Closed: 12 August 1963 Steeplehouse–Friden (including Middleton incline)
9 April 1967 Cromford–Steeplehouse closed (including Sheep Pasture incline).
2 October 1967 Friden–Parsley Hay
21 November 1967 Parsley Hay–Hindlow

Left:
Pictured on 18 May 1964, this view of the Cromford incline shows well the nature of the cable-operated sections. *R. C. Riley*

Top:
One of the ex-North London Railway 0-6-0Ts, No 58856 is pictured at Friden with a joint SLS/MLS special to the High Peak in April 1953. *J. Davenport/Colour-Rail (BRM545)*

Above:
Nos 58860 and 58850 blast up Hopton incline with an enthusiasts' special on 25 September 1955. Built at the North London Railway's Bow Works to an 1879 design of J. C. Park, a number of the 0-6-0Ts were transferred to the Cromford & High Peak line. *Eric Russell/Colour-Rail*

Left:
Although this is a springtime photograph – taken in May 1966 – of rakes of full and empty mineral wagons, by this date the Cromford & High Peak was in the autumn of its life; in less than 18 months scenes such as this would be a thing of the past. *R. C. Riley*

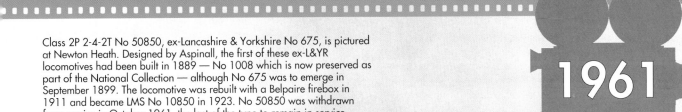

Class 2P 2-4-2T No 50850, ex-Lancashire & Yorkshire No 675, is pictured at Newton Heath. Designed by Aspinall, the first of these ex-L&YR locomotives had been built in 1889 — No 1008 which is now preserved as part of the National Collection — although No 675 was to emerge in September 1899. The locomotive was rebuilt with a Belpaire firebox in 1911 and became LMS No 10850 in 1923. No 50850 was withdrawn from service in October 1961, the last of the type to remain in service.
John Adams/Colour-Rail

1961

The Last Train from Bala to Blaenau Ffestiniog

Part of the fascination of railways is that every aspect can be enjoyed and studied in a variety of ways. Enthusiasts were often chief among mourners of branch closures, especially after they were accelerated by the Beeching Report.

Broadly, they chose their own ways of saying farewell to lines which they had travelled for years or, with closure pending, were using for the first and last time.

Those who prized a last chance to remember a branch as they knew it — and also preferred comfort to crush — caught service trains a day or two ahead of withdrawal. Generally, they found they had the trains almost to themselves.

Crowd-conditioned enthusiasts often revelled in unique carnival-to-gloom atmospheres of last-day services, and especially those on the last train of the evening. Most popular of all were last specials organised on the day after official closure to passengers.

None of those conditions applied to the last train over the Arenig mountains between Bala and Blaenau Ffestiniog, a single branch which reached 1,200ft above sea level at Cwm Prysor. The Midland Area of the Stephenson Locomotive Society special did not run until Sunday 22 January 1961 — just over a *year* after the last regular passenger train. The occasion was unusual because the branch never had a Sunday service.

Another W. A. 'Cam' Camwell-inspired tour produced a Sunday working over weekday-only passenger lines in December 1962. It was the equally-memorable 'Farewell to the Brecon Lines' special over the Mid-Wales Railway between Moat Lane and Brecon and the Midland route east to Hereford. Both passenger services had been withdrawn the previous day.

The Blaenau Ffestiniog special ran a few days ahead of complete closure of most of the 25-mile route. Passenger trains continued to reach Bala from Bala Junction on the former GWR secondary route between Ruabon and Morfa Mawddach until slightly premature closure three years later.

Because of flooding in the Dee Valley, Ruabon–Bala Junction closed on 13 December 1964, rather than 18 January 1965. That prevented a proper valedictory tour by the SLS, whose 'Farewell to the Cambrian Railways' ran over the Llanfyllin branch instead.

The Blaenau Ffestiniog branch closed so that Liverpool Corporation could build Tryweryn Reservoir by submerging part of the trackbed. The branch was among the remotest in North Wales. The GWR described the district as 'wild and rugged' and warned staff to keep a close watch on the line in winter to prevent it becoming blocked by snowdrifts.

The largest station was among the hills at Trawsfynydd, where platforms, sidings and a troop yard were added after the Army established an artillery camp in 1903. Associated with the branch closure was a standard gauge link-up at Blaenau Ffestiniog in 1964 with the former LNWR Conwy Valley branch to allow trains carrying nuclear flasks to reach a siding at Trawsfynydd close to a small power station.

Reading
Southern, D. W., *Bala Junction to Blaenau Ffestiniog*

Bala–Blaenau Ffestiniog

Distance: 24¾ miles
Owner: Great Western Railway
Opened: 1 November 1882 Bala Junction (new station)–Ffestiniog
10 September 1883 Ffestiniog–Blaenau Ffestiniog
Closed: 4 January 1960 Bala–Blaenau Ffestiniog for Passengers
28 January 1961 Bala–Blaenau Ffestiniog for Goods
2 November 1964 Bala Junction–Bala for Goods
18 January 1965 Bala Junction–Bala for Passengers

Ruabon–Morfa Mawddach
Distance: 52¼ miles
Owner: Great Western Railway
Opened: 1861–1869
Closed: 1964–1965

Left:
On 22 January 1961, a year after scheduled passenger services over the line had been withdrawn, the SLS operated a final special over the Bala-Blaenau Ffestiniog route prior to its complete closure (on 30 January 1961). The train was headed by Pannier tanks Nos 4645 and 8781, and the pair is seen here at Bala, amongst the typical throng on these occasions, waiting to depart. *Colour-Rail*

Above right:
Still with 'GWR' visible on the side of its tank, '74xx' 0-6-0PT takes water at Trawsfynydd whilst heading a single-coach train towards Blaenau Ffestiniog in April 1959. *Gavin Morrison/Colour-Rail (BRW1200)*

Right:
'87xx' class 0-6-0PT No 5774 is caught at Blaenau Ffestiniog Central with a local for Bala in August 1955. Following closure of the line through to Bala, the section to Trawsfynydd was retained to serve the nuclear power station there. The power station has now closed, leaving the future of the remaining section of this erstwhile GWR route uncertain. *J. B. Snell/Colour-Rail (BRW847)*

London Transport Steam and Electric

Much of the modernisation carried out during the *Railway Roundabout* years was unique. Never again, for instance, will there be wholesale replacement of steam by diesel and electric traction.

The sequence about London Transport showed an unusual aspect with steam being given a fresh lease of life. It happened because, after many branches closed, British Railways was left with a surplus of pannier tanks. To reduce it a little, 13 were sold to London Transport for use on engineers' and other works trains.

In May 1961 one was busy at LT Neasden depot, where it was joined in 'shunts past' the camera by two veterans which LT inherited from the Metropolitan Railway.

These were an 0-6-2 tank and a far more handsome 0-4-4 tank, which was MR No 1. It was preserved after withdrawal in 1964 and has since made occasional forays with special trains run over LT metals.

Neasden depot was then taking delivery in preparation for trials of the first of LT's unpainted aluminium electric units. They were destined for the Circle and Metropolitan lines following the 6½-mile extension of electrification north from Rickmansworth to Amersham, and also of the Chesham branch. This also led to the withdrawal of all LT services to Aylesbury.

Electrification had taken place in September 1960, bringing to an end locomotive changing at Rickmansworth which, Professor H. P. White claimed in *Regional History of Railways, Volume 3 Greater London*, was the fastest in the world.

It did not seem to be quite like that when Bo-Bo No 8 *Sherlock Holmes* took over a train of Dreadnought coaches from a Fairburn 2-6-4 tank. All the electric locomotives bore names. Today, No 12 *Sarah Siddons* is perhaps the best known because it occasionally hauls special trains.

A fleet of 20 Bo-Bos had hauled trains to Rickmansworth since third-rail electrification of the main line out of Baker Street was extended from Harrow in 1925.

This was in an era when the Metropolitan was enticing Londoners to move out of town by developing Metroland where, in the 1920s, one of its subsidiary companies built over 4,000 houses on new estates between Neasden and Amersham.

The Metropolitan Railway became part of the London Passenger Transport Board in 1933 and four years later the LNER took over the working of trains north of Rickmansworth. The Metropolitan's main-line locomotives were taken into LNER stock while LT kept some of its older locomotives for engineering operations.

Reading

Gillham, J. C., *The Age of the Electric Train*
Casserley, H. C., *Britain's Joint Lines*

London Baker Street–Amersham

Distance:	23½ miles
Owner:	Metropolitan Railway
Opened:	Baker Street–Rickmansworth 1868–1887
	Chesham branch 1889 (3 miles)
	Amersham and Aylesbury 1892.
Electrification:	Progressively. Harrow–Rickmansworth
	1925. Rickmansworth–Amersham/
	Chesham branch 1960

Below:
'F' class 0-6-2T No L52 was built for the Metropolitan Railway in 1901 by the Yorkshire Engine Co (Works No 627) as No 93. It was one of four of the type taken over by the LPTB in 1933 (as Nos L49-L52) and was the last to be withdrawn (in July 1964). It is pictured at Neasden in May 1961. *John Adams/Colour-Rail (LT24)*

Above right:
Now preserved and restored to its original Metropolitan number (No 1), London Transport No L44 was an 'E' class 0-4-4T built by the Metropolitan itself at Neasden Works (one of only three locomotives constructed there) in September 1898. It was withdrawn in March 1964 and is now to be seen at Quainton Road, where it forms part of the collection of the Buckinghamshire Railway Centre. It was recorded at Neasden in May 1961. *John Adams/Colour-Rail (LT21)*

Below right:
A general view of Neasden power station sees No L53 shuffling into position during April 1957. No L53 was originally Metropolitan Railway No 101 and was a Peckett 0-6-0ST (Works No 664) delivered in March 1897. It was withdrawn from service in August 1960. *L. V. Reason/Colour-Rail (LT137)*

Swindon Engines

Why was the Great Western Railway called 'God's Wonderful Railway'? Enthusiasts too young to remember it in its heyday may find part of the answer in this sequence of three veterans being shunted at Swindon Works. For it had magnificent locomotives which were a delight to behold!

Just how much so I remember from spotting days at Chester in wartime when all of the four types on parade at Swindon Works worked in and out of the north end of the General station. So did a host of LMS locomotives of which the most distinguished were unrebuilt 'Royal Scot' class 4-6-0s, which always looked more powerful than they did after they were rebuilt.

But it was GWR locomotives that looked the most majestic at Chester, especially 'Star' class 4-6-0s arriving and departing with Birkenhead–Paddington expresses. These were worked by other types of locomotives north of Chester.

With their double frames, wheelbarrow tenders and almost open footplates, 'Bulldog' class 4-4-0s caught the eye far more quickly than locomotives of similar size like LMS Class 2P 4-4-0s which headed North Wales stopping trains. Their modern profile was in sharp contrast to the 'Bulldogs', whose 'ancient' appearance suggested that only the demands of war had saved them from a scrapheap.

Part of the fascination of railways is their ability to evoke strong memories such as the sight of a 'Bulldog' half a century after seeing them at work. The first footplate I boarded on a locomotive in steam was that of Chester-shedded No 3366. How grateful I was to the driver, held at Birkenhead Town down-starter while running light engine to Birkenhead Woodside, who took pity on a young spotter by offering him a warm place before an open firebox door on a bitter winter morning.

Birkenhead Town was a quiet station, with both platforms in a cutting. But on walking out of the booking hall passengers saw the towering cranes and sheds of the Cammell Laird shipyard where, on that day of 1942, thousands of men were building warships.

Much of the steel for those vessels reached the shipyard by rail on trains hauled by locomotives far bigger than 'Bulldogs' or 'Dean Goods'. Chester GWR shed had an allocation, although sometimes it was of no more than a single engine. The 'Deans' are more traditionally associated with the old Cambrian Railways and GWR lines on the Welsh border where they epitomised the motive power of country branches.

A high profile publicity machine served the GWR so well that its image lived on after Nationalisation, and helped to keep the Western Region different from other Regions. (Another factor was the adoption by the Western Region of diesel-hydraulic rather than diesel-electric locomotives.)

In 1938 the company published a handbook which became a classic: *GWR Engines, Names, Numbers, Types, Classes etc.* Despite a reprint the same year, stocks were exhausted early in World War 2. By the time a third edition was published in 1946, the author, W. G. Chapman, noted that it had become evident 'that the interest evinced in the subject by large numbers of railway enthusiasts had in no way diminished'.

Below:
Looking superb with its rake of carmine and cream coaches, ex-GWR 4-4-0 No 3440 *City of Truro*, by reputation the first steam locomotive to exceed 100mph, was photographed at Swindon on 16 June 1957. Constructed at Swindon in 1903, No 3440 was withdrawn (as No 3717) in 1931 and transferred to the old railway museum in York for preservation. The locomotive was returned to active service for use on specials in 1957 before being withdrawn again in 1961. It now forms part of the National Collection and can be seen on display at the National Railway Museum in York. *Eric Russell/Colour-Rail*

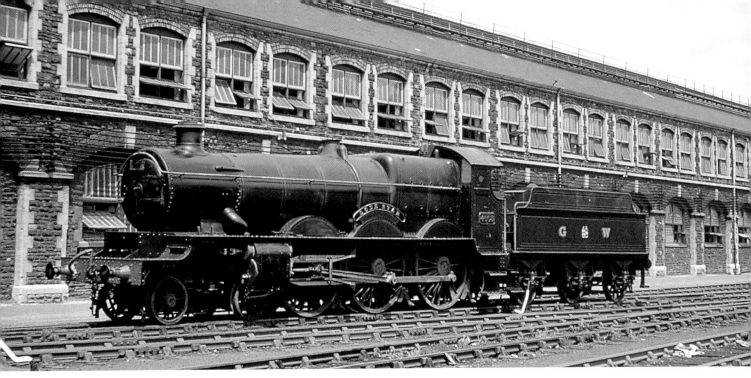

No 4003 *Lode Star*, which headed its class in that handbook, and 'Dean Goods' No 2516 are part of the National Railway Museum collection.

The Great Western Railway Museum at Swindon, where these locomotives are sometimes housed, is in the heart of Brunel's railway village. It was built as a lodging house for railway workers and became a Wesleyan Methodist chapel before being acquired by the Borough Council.

Introducing a 1971 edition of the Museum handbook, L. T. C. Rolt felt that no visitor 'can remain unmoved by the exhibits on view, large or small, quaint or commonplace; reminders of illustrious engineers or of obscure men whose routine jobs kept the trains running'.

Reading
Allen, G. Freeman, *The Western Since 1948*

Above:
'Star' class 4-6-0 No 4003 *Lode Star* is pictured outside Swindon Works in 1954. The locomotive, one of 73 of the four-cylinder design, was built at Swindon in February 1907. By the date of this photograph, No 4003 had been withdrawn from service (in July 1951) and had been preserved. The last of the 'Star' class to remain operational was No 4056 *Princess Margaret*, which was withdrawn in October 1957. No 4003 is now displayed at the Great Western Museum in Swindon. *Colour-Rail (BRW12)*

Below:
A total of 260 'Dean Goods' 0-6-0s were constructed by the Great Western Railway between May 1883 and January 1899. Of these only some 53 remained in service at Nationalisation. The first withdrawals had taken place as early as the first decade of the 20th century; the last almost 50 years later. Numerous examples of the type saw war service in both world wars, many ending their days in France and elsewhere, well away from their traditional haunts. The penultimate example of the class to be withdrawn was No 2516, which was claimed for the National Collection when withdrawn in May 1956. It is seen here at Swindon, where it is now preserved in the town's Railway Museum. *Colour-Rail*

The Ravenglass & Eskdale Railway

Often it is useful to get a dispassionate view of a railway to find out how it might be regarded outside the cloistered, biased world of the enthusiast. To do that I turned to the recently published *A Literary Guide to the Lake District* by Grevel Lindop. He feels that the R&ER 'provides an exhilarating ride through magnificent scenery'.

An introductory quote to his book is Arnold Bennett's description of the Lakes being 'a hell of a way from London'. Pat and John found they were a long way from Birmingham when they drove to the R&ER, 'Ratty' as it is affectionately known.

The isolation of West Cumbria was even acknowledged in Victorian *Bradshaw's*. Summer tourists in 1885 found a footnote to the railway's entry stating that the terminus at Boot at the head of Eskdale was 14 miles from Keswick 'by foot'.

To get to Ravenglass, the *Railway Roundabout* team used Britain's first stretch of motorway, the newly-opened Preston Bypass on what is now the M6.

In recent years it has been doubled to eight lanes. The R&ER has remained single, but it thrives, advertising itself in the *Great Britain Passenger Railway Timetable* as 'England's oldest steam-operated narrow gauge railway' and adding that it 'runs through glorious scenery to the foot of Lakeland's highest hills'.

If I write with affection about 'Ratty' — the only major narrow gauge line in the Lake District — it is because my

first live BBC radio broadcast was about it being put up for sale in the late 1950s.

The fortunes of the railway were boosted in the late 1970s and early 1980s when BR revived steam in Cumbria with the summer 'Cumbrian Coast Express'. Locomotives including *Flying Scotsman* worked to Sellafield.

A stop was made at Ravenglass with enough time for tourists to make a round trip to Boot. After making one in 1983, I returned to Ravenglass, listened to the gentle hiss of Paddy Smith's 'Black Five', No 5407, rejoined the 'Cumbrian Coast Pullman' and realised how much poorer West Cumbria would be without its railways. I recalled that while the 'Ratty's' future was in the balance, BR withdrew passenger services from the scenically attractive Coniston branch. One of its memorials is to be found at Ravenglass: the old footbridge from the branch terminal.

Reading

Broughton, J. and Harris, N., *British Railways Past and Present No 1 Cumbria*
Davies, W. J. K., *The Ravenglass & Eskdale Railway*
Norman, K. J., *The Furness Railway: A Recollection*
Whitehouse, P. B., *Narrow Gauge Album*

Ravenglass–Boot

Distance:	7 miles
Owner:	Ravenglass & Eskdale Railway
Gauge:	3ft 0in
Opened:	1875–76
Closed:	30 April 1913
Gauge:	15in
Reopened:	1915–17
	Offered for sale 1958
Operators:	Ravenglass & Eskdale Railway Company Ltd from March 1961

Left:
Oldest of the 'Ratty's' operational fleet is the 0-8-2 *River Irt*, which was built by Heywood in 1894. It is seen here at, appropriately, Irton Road at the head of an RCTS special over the line. *Colour-Rail*

Above right:
With the peaks of the Lake District forming a dramatic backdrop — and few will forget the approach to the 'Ratty' from the east over Hard Knott Pass — No 9 *River Mite* departs from Boot with a service towards Ravenglass. No 9, a 2-8-2, was built by Clarksons in 1966 (Works No 4669). *Colour-Rail*

Right:
River Esk, a 2-8-2 built by Davey Paxman in 1923, is pictured at Dalegarth in 1960. *Colour-Rail*

A Goods Train: Bath to Evercreech Junction

Edward Beal, who wrote a superb book, *The Craft of Modelling Railways* in 1937, quoted the American writer O. Henry who said that to be really happy in this world, you must have 'a little country where you don't live'.

I found this to be true every time I got up before dawn to work on BBC Breakfast Television. Before leaving home, I used to snatch five minutes to read a book over breakfast. For years the book that took me into my 'little country' was *The Somerset & Dorset: An English Cross-Country Railway* by Ivo Peters, published in 1974. That was seven years after closure when *The Times* had noted: 'After 111 years the curtains have come down, but the legend of the Somerset and Dorset is not likely to be forgotten in the West Country.'

The line became so much of a legend that it has since found its own niche in railway history. Its legendary status is due partly to Ivo Peters and to his wonderful photographic record of the system over many years. After he died in 1989 a road in Bath was named in his honour.

The third largest of Britain's Joint Railways, the S&D was full of individuality and character. It was Midland and London & South Western Joint until Grouping and then LMS and SR. In *Bradshaw's* and other passenger timetables, its main line was shown as 71 miles between Bath Queen Square station, renamed Green Park by BR, and Bournemouth West, but the Joint line metals ended at Broadstone, 8 miles short of Bournemouth.

The film was shot on the most spectacular stretch: the Bath Extension of 26 miles between Bath and Evercreech Junction, which took the main line over the Mendip Hills. The summit at Masbury, 817ft above sea level, was flanked by long gradients of up to 1 in 50. It was double-heading of heavy holiday expresses that attracted enthusiasts to the lineside. With local road knowledge, some were able to photograph the same train four times on a single journey. The *Railway Roundabout* approach was different. Its aim was not to show the glamour of the S&D but rather techniques of operation.

The S&D was the first railway in Britain to introduce automatic apparatus for tablet exchanging at speed on single lines. This invention of Alfred Whitaker, the company's Locomotive Superintendent, was later used on other lines including the Midland & Great Northern.

BR provided facilities on a morning goods from Bath, hauled by one of the S&D 2-8-0s which the Midland built specially for the line. Two types were introduced in 1914 and 1925. In the final years, BR used even more powerful locomotives: Class 9F 2-10-0s. Sometimes they were coupled with the veteran 2-8-0s, forming the most powerful locomotive combination ever used on the S&D.

The 'Pines Express' between Bournemouth and Manchester and Liverpool, the best remembered crack express over the route, gave passengers plenty of time to view the scenery, occupying the Bath Extension for about an hour. The run down of the S&D prior to closure began with the diversion of the 'Pines Express' to the Reading–Southampton route. Today, still named in timetables, it connects Manchester and Bournemouth in about five hours — some two hours quicker than when it pounded the Mendips.

S&D: 'Slow and Dirty' or 'Swift and Delightful'. Views of the S&D were always mixed, yet as David St John Thomas wrote in his *Regional History of Railways: Volume 1 The West Country*, 'To live on the Somerset & Dorset was a romantic distinction'.

Reading
Casserley, H. C., *Britain's Joint Lines*

Bath Green Park–Evercreech Junction

Distance: 26 miles
Owner: Somerset & Dorset Joint Railway
Opened: 20 July 1874
Closed: 6 March 1966

Below left:
Ex-Somerset & Dorset 2-8-0 No 53807 makes a dramatic entry into Masbury station with an up freight. No 53807 was one of the second batch of S&D 2-8-0s to be built — by Robert Stephenson — and was constructed during 1925.
Colour-Rail (SD165)

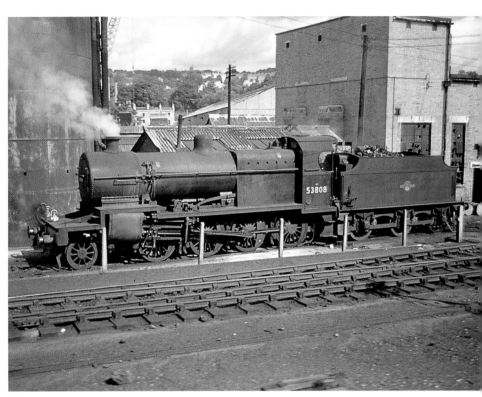

Right:
Pictured at Bath Green Park on 7 September 1962, '7F' No 53808 was one of 11 2-8-0s delivered to the Somerset & Dorset Joint Railway. The first six, built by the Midland Railway at Derby, were delivered in 1914, the remaining five, built by Robert Stephenson, arrived in 1925. No 53808 (as S&D No 88) was one of the second batch. Withdrawn in 1964, it was one of two of the type to pass via Woodham Bros's scrapyard into preservation. It is now to be seen on the West Somerset Railway. *Colour-Rail*

Below:
Although the S&D acquired six of the LMS 'Jinty' 0-6-0s in 1928/29, BR No 47496 was not one of them. The locomotive is seen at Midsomer Norton on 17 August 1962. *Colour-Rail*

Lancashire & Yorkshire Special

For years, enthusiasts visited North West England to travel on passenger trains which regularly climbed steep inclines or to watch goods trains pounding them.

The most spectacular and exciting ascents were those made by locomotives rushing the banks on the Cromford & High Peak. But enthusiasts were also attracted to four inclines which the Lancashire & Yorkshire Railway listed as having its severest gradients: 1 in 34 to the summit of the entire system near Shawforth on the Rochdale–Bacup branch; 1 in 40 near Accrington and Padiham in North East Lancashire, and the Werneth, or Oldham, Incline.

It formed part of the first railway between Manchester and Oldham. Graded at 1 in 27 for three quarters of a mile it was among the steepest in Britain to be used by regular passenger trains.

It shared the honour with the Holywell Junction to Holywell Town branch in North Wales. It had a far shorter life, being opened by the LNWR in 1912 and closed in autumn 1954.

The Werneth Incline was opened by the Manchester & Leeds Railway in 1842 and rope-worked until 1851. It was displaced as the main line between Manchester and Oldham when a more easily graded route was opened from Newton Heath in North Manchester to the top of the incline at Werneth in 1880.

It was used by the majority of local passenger services and today it carries an Oldham–Rochdale circular service from Manchester Victoria. Trains, often Class 142 'Pacers', introduced locally in summer 1985, make their first stop at Dean Lane, 2½ miles from Victoria, which was one of the stations used by generations of locomotive men to get to and from Newton Heath, its largest shed, which the 'Lanky'

always listed as No 1. It was built in the 'V' of the Oldham and Rochdale lines.

Once it had a staff of more than 1,000 men and its allocation of over 200 locomotives included every type it built or owned. The L&YR locomotive works were at Horwich near Bolton, but Newton Heath was the site of the carriage and wagon works where it built and repaired all its own vehicles.

In 1961, enthusiasts of the Roch Valley Society began a railtour which started from the adjacent carriage sidings and climbed Werneth Incline, which was then in decline between the end of regular passenger services in June 1958 and complete closure after goods services ceased in October 1963.

The Incline track was lifted soon afterwards but representatives of both classes of locomotives which hauled the special have survived. 0-6-0 No 52322, which was among 180 of the class listed in the summer 1953 *abc of British Railways Locomotives*, has been preserved and in 1996 I saw it still on ex-L&YR territory at the East Lancashire Railway shed at Bury.

The first of the class of more than 300 L&YR 2-4-2 tanks is part of the National Collection, repainted in its old 'Lanky' livery and numbered L&YR No 1008. An enthusiast who remembered the 2-4-2 tanks from the mid-1920s was Canon Roger Lloyd who went to Newton Heath as a young curate. In *Farewell to Steam* he recalled them passing the vicarage on the Oldham line. 'They were midgets of great versatility and surprising strength... But when you had seen one of them you had seen them all.'

Reading
Marshall, John, *The Lancashire & Yorkshire Railway,*
Volumes 1–3

Middleton Junction–Oldham Werneth

Distance: 1¾ miles
Owner: Lancashire & Yorkshire Railway
Opened: 31 March 1842
Closed: 9 June 1958 for Passengers
       11 October 1963 for Goods

Left:
Ex-L&YR veterans Nos 52271 and 50850 attack the steep Werneth Incline near Oldham in September 1960. *Patrick Whitehouse/Colour-Rail*

Above right:
In 1877 the L&YR introduced a batch of 0-6-0s designed by Barton Wright; these were rebuilt as saddle tanks on the instructions of Aspinall from 1891 onwards. Built by Kitson, No 51371 was constructed in October 1878 as L&YR No 164. Rebuilt in December 1893, No 164 became LMS No 11371 at the Grouping. By this time No 51371 — seen here at Newton Heath — was approaching the end of its operational life, being withdrawn in March 1961.
Eric Russell/Colour-Rail

Right:
One of the numerous Aspinall-designed 0-6-0s, No 52271, also seen at Newton Heath, was built in December 1894 as L&YR No 270. Becoming LMS No 12271 in 1923, No 52271 was to survive until August 1961.
John Adams/Colour-Rail

The Welsh Narrow Gauge

Three narrow gauge lines of North and mid-Wales, all with close associations with the Cambrian Coast line, were visited during an era of transition when they were developing and expanding after World War 2.

Since 1961, the Talyllyn Railway has extended from Abergynolwyn to a cosy terminus tucked into a wooded hillside at Nant Gwernol. The Vale of Rheidol has lost its roundabout exit from Aberystwyth beside the river and incorporated its terminus into the main line station. And the Festiniog (sic) is back at Blaenau, a useful and attractive link between the Conwy Valley branch and the Cambrian Coast line.

After the war, the character of the lines changed, notably through the withdrawal of goods services and exploiting them as attractions for tourists, who travel because they want to travel. A century and more ago the lines carried men to and from work.

Bradshaw's of summer 1885 showed the first Tal-y-Llyn (sic) trains of the morning from Pendre station at Towyn and Abergynolwyn as Monday only 'Workmen's Trains. Will not run when any stoppage occurs at the Bryneglwys Quarries'.

Workers who had to get up before dawn to catch those trains and then sit for 40min during a 6¾-mile journey, might be forgiven for not appreciating the railway in the way that tourists do today.

On the Festiniog at that time, the first morning departure from Portmadoc for Duffws, a 2min journey beyond the main station at Blaenau Ffestiniog, was shown as a government service.

All three little railways served areas of great scenic beauty and the railways did what they could to get people to see them, but their tourist potential was limited because they were too isolated to be reached on day trips from big towns or cities and accommodation was very limited for those wanting to stay a few days in areas like Snowdonia.

On 23 July 1879, Thomas Wildgoose wrote his name in a copy of the latest edition of *The Gossiping Guide to Wales*. It is doubtful if he used it much for his copy is in excellent condition with the gold-lettered cover and spine still bright.

The large amount of information about railways given in the guide reflected their importance to tourism. It was stated that the line from Machynlleth to Corris was conveying passengers and that 'A 2ft 6inch gauge railroad now runs from Towyn to Abergynolwyn, which, though chiefly for the conveyance of slates, accommodates passengers as well'.

Several pages are devoted to 'The Toy Railway to Festiniog', one verdict of the author being that the town of Ffestiniog was connected with the rest of the world by a wonderful little line which was serving as a model in every civilized spot.

There is, of course, no mention of the Vale of Rheidol Railway, not opened until nearly a quarter of a century later. Serving only a valley, it lacked the potential of the Festiniog Railway. It owes its survival to being championed by Aberystwyth Borough Council as a major tourist attraction.

In the 1950s it came near to closure because of lack of passengers: in summer 1954 it carried less than 17,000. But after extensive publicity campaigns, passenger totals built up gradually. In 1966 they reached over 46,000. The following year the VOR was reprieved by British Railways to become, after the official end of steam in 1968, BR's only steam line. It held that distinction until passing into the private ownership of the Brecon Steam Railway.

Reading
Boyd, J. I .C., *Narrow Gauge Railways in Mid-Wales*
Butcher, A. C., *Railways Restored*, Ian Allan Publishing
Whitehouse, P. B., *Narrow Gauge Album*

Portmadoc–Blaenau Ffestiniog

Distance:	13½ miles
Owner:	Festiniog Railway Company
Gauge:	1ft 11½ in.
Opened:	1836 for Goods; 1865 for Passengers
Closed:	1939–46
Reopened:	From July 1955

Tywyn Wharf–Nant Gwernol

Distance:	7½ miles
Gauge:	2ft 3in
Owner:	Talyllyn Railway Company
Opened:	1865

Aberystwyth–Devil's Bridge

Distance:	11¾ miles
Owner:	Brecon Mountain Railway
Gauge:	1ft 11½in
Opened:	1902
Closed:	mid-1920s for Goods

Below left:
Vale of Rheidol No 7 *Owain Glyndwr* is pictured at Devil's Bridge in September 1958 at the head of a rake of chocolate and cream painted coaches. *DBW/Colour-Rail*

Right:
Talyllyn No 1 *Talyllyn* was built by Fletcher Jennings & Co in 1865 (Works No 42). This 0-4-2ST is seen at Pendre in 1960. *Eric Russell/Colour-Rail*

Below:
Two of the Festiniog Railway's unique double-Fairlies are seen at Porthmadoc in 1960. On the left is *Earl of Merioneth* whilst on the right is *Merddin Emrys*. The latter, No 10, was built by the Festiniog itself at Boston Lodge in 1879. The former, as *Livingston Thompson*, emerged from Boston Lodge seven years later. It was renamed *Earl of Merioneth* for a period; the title is one held by HRH the Duke of Edinburgh. More recently the locomotive has reverted to its original name and a new *Earl of Merioneth* has been built. *Livingston Thompson* is currently on loan to the National Railway Museum. *Colour-Rail*

Southern Region Engines

How little things can trigger memories of years ago! It happened when a friend, Nigel Payton, who has helped with several of my books, noted my home postcode ended 'SR' and scribbled a PS to a letter stating: 'I was at school at Sherborne. I greatly admired the "King Arthurs".'

The 4-6-0s are seen here, but the Southern Railway, which disappeared on Nationalisation, will be best remembered for its highly original Pacifics, which lacked the grace and beauty of the Gresley 'A4s', but had a tremendous sense of power.

The *abc of Southern Locomotives*, written by Ian Allan, appeared in the middle of World War 2 in December 1942. The seventh edition in June 1945, took the total production of the *abc* series to over three quarters of a million in three years. The seventh edition caught both the growing excitement of spotters and the urgency facing the publisher to try to satisfy their demands.

'Even though the introduction to the Southern of further 'Merchant Navy' class locos as well as a new design of lightweight 4-6-2s to be known as the 'West Country' class is imminent, it is felt that we can no longer delay the production of this edition.'

The cover featured an artist's impression of one of the streamlined 'Merchant Navy' class 4-6-2s, No 21C8 *Orient Line*. The numbering was explained in a leaflet which O. V. Bulleid, their designer, produced on the introduction of the slightly smaller 'Battle of Britain' class.

'They are numbered in the 21C100 series, which shows the engine number and wheel arrangement. The number of driving axles is indicated by the corresponding letter of the alphabet eg "C" for three. The first numeral indicates the number of carrying axles in front of the driving wheels, and the second number of such axles behind the drivers. The number after the capital letter is that of the engine in the class.'

The Pacifics were painted in the Southern's peacetime livery of malachite green with yellow lining.

In that livery they must have looked far smarter than the locomotives seen in the 'shunt-past' at Nine Elms depot. On parade were veterans displaced by the Kent Coast electrification being transferred to the South West to replace even older locomotives.

After final days in the West, the locomotives went for scrap, but the former Southern Railway and its predecessors are well represented in the ranks of locomotives retired to the National Collection at York or to a number of preserved railways.

No 30937 *Epsom* was scrapped in 1962, but Maunsell's most powerful class of British 4-4-0 is represented at the National Railway Museum by No 925 *Cheltenham*, again in malachite green.

York is also the home of a 4-4-0 of infinite grace: No 737, survivor of a Wainwright South Eastern & Chatham design turned out at Ashford in the year King Edward VII succeeded Queen Victoria. It was among locomotives taken into Southern Railway stock at Grouping and transferred to British Railways on Nationalisation.

Rebuilt 'Merchant Navy' No 35029 *Ellerman Lines* was 'rebuilt' again after withdrawal, being sectionalised proving perhaps that the beauty of steam locomotives is only skin deep! It is a testimony to how successful many locomotive designers were in hiding a mass of ugly tubes and chambers including fire and smokeboxes.

A host of pleasing designs were turned out by the London Brighton & South Coast from its works at Brighton. They celebrated a century of locomotive building in the early 1950s and continued the work for several more years.

A standard Class 4 2-6-4 tank, which brought construction to an end in 1957, also brings to an end the 1961 video tape.

The Kent Coast electrification which devastated the Southern Region steam locomotive fleet took place in two stages: from Gillingham to Ramsgate and from Canterbury to Dover Marina in summer 1959 and from Sevenoaks to the coast three years later. The scheme gave the Southern Region another 200 miles of electrified routes.

Reading
Dendy Marshall, C. F., *History of the Southern Railway*
Gillham, J. C., *The Age of the Electric Train*

Left:
Unrebuilt 'West Country' No 34094 *Mortehoe* with original tender awaits its next turn of duty at Nine Elms in October 1956. Built in October 1949 after Nationalisation, No 34094 was never rebuilt, being withdrawn from Eastleigh shed in August 1964. T. J. Edgington/Colour-Rail (BRS645)

Above right:
'Schools' class 4-4-0 No 30911 *Dover* is also pictured at Nine Elms, but three years later in September 1959. T. J. Edgington/Colour-Rail (BRS725)

Right:
This superb panoramic shot of Brighton Shed sees a variety of ex-Southern Railway motive power on 1 September 1961. Locomotives visible include 'West Country' Pacific No 34100 *Appledore*, 'Q' class 0-6-0 No 30533 and 'E4' class 0-6-2T No 32503. Coded by BR, Brighton shed closed to steam in 1964. *Colour-Rail*

Severn & Wye Railway

Oil paintings reproduced on the jackets of railway books published decades ago still give deep and lasting pleasure to enthusiasts. Some will pay several times the original price of the book just to enjoy the scene on the jacket.

Two books which are among a miniature picture-gallery on my bookshelves are of widely distanced and contrasting scenes. A classic C. Hamilton Ellis oil painting of a North British train at Crianlarich station in Edwardian days as spring melts the snows on the surrounding Highlands, introduces the author's own history of The North British Railway. It was first published by Ian Allan Publishing in 1955.

The second, of a scene deep in the Forest of Dean in late Victorian days, is the work of Hugh M. Crowther. A Severn & Wye Railway diminutive tank, *Maid Marian*, heads a train of two coaches calling at Lower Lydbrook after crossing a striking viaduct which dominated the Wye Valley until demolition in May 1966. The painting forms the jacket and frontispiece of *The Severn & Wye Railway*, by Harry Paar, first published by David & Charles in 1963.

Lydbrook was just under two miles from the northern end of the Severn & Wye Joint Railway and its junction with the Ross & Monmouth Railway.

In 1961, a push-pull railtour with a second ex-GWR pannier tank sandwiched between the three coaches, helped members of the Stephenson Locomotive Society recapture the spirit and special flavour of the railways of the Forest. Their legacy, active and expanding, is the preserved Dean Forest Railway between Lydney Town and Parkend.

The short section once formed part of the single track 'main line' of the Severn & Wye Joint Railway or Line — both descriptions were used officially by the owners — the Great Western and London Midland & Scottish Railways.

It ran from the former Midland Railway Bristol & Gloucester main line at Berkeley Road, to Lydbrook Junction. Its outstanding feature was the Severn Railway Bridge near Sharpness. It was partly destroyed by a small ship in October 1960 when it was being strengthened to take heavier locomotives to create an alternative route between South Wales, the Midlands and Bristol. It was never rebuilt.

The accident led to the abrupt end of passenger services over the nine miles between Berkeley Road and Lydney Town via Sharpness, but the railtour was able to cover the 3½ miles from Lydney Town to the disused Severn Bridge station, shown in timetables as that for Blakeney.

Despite the curtailment, the railtour was of exceptional interest because it ran north from Lydney Town to Cinderford and over the Coleford branch from Parkend. They were lines from which passenger services had been withdrawn in summer 1929.

However, Cinderford retained a passenger service over the ex-GWR branch from Newnham until November 1958.

Double-pannier power was required on the 3½-mile Coleford branch because of the gradients. It climbed a long stretch at 1 in 30 from the junction to Milkwall and then dropped to the town at 1 in 47. Little wonder that there was a sand drag at Coleford Junction and that working instructions

laid down that 'No wagon with a defective brake must, under any circumstances, be allowed to work on the Branch'.

In the 1950s, the Forest was acknowledged as bus territory by the Western Region. Berkeley Road–Lydney Town passenger timetables (which showed weekday only, second-class only trains), stated that bus services operated between Coleford and Ross-on-Wye; Lydney, Monmouth and Lydbrook.

Reading
Casserley, H. C., *Britain's Joint Lines*
Paar, H. W., *The Severn & Wye Railway*
The Great Western Railway in the Forest of Dean
Pope, I., How, B., Karau, P., *Severn & Wye Railway, Volumes 1 and 2*
Smith, P., *An Historical Survey of the Forest of Dean Railways Layouts and Illustrations*

| **Berkeley Road–Cinderford** | |
Coleford Junction–Cinderford (S&WJ)	
Distance:	18¾ miles (Berkeley Road–Cinderford); 3¾ miles (Coleford Junction–Cinderford)
Opened:	1874–79
Closed:	8 July 1929 Lydney Town–Lydbrook Junction; Coleford branch: Coleford Junction–Cinderford (S&WJ) for Passengers. 25 October 1960 Severn Railway Bridge severed; Lydney Town–Berkeley Road closed to through passenger services. The S&WJ closed completely in several sections. BR took Lydney–Parkend out of use in 1976.
Reopened:	The Dean Forest Railway now open from Norchard, north of Lydney, via St Mary's Halt to Lydney Junction.

Above:
Class 87xx 0-6-0PT No 8701 is seen at Coleford with the special tour that ran over the Forest of Dean lines on 13 May 1961. *Colour-Rail*

Left:
'87xx' No 8701, with it headboard, on the left and '64xx' 0-6-0PT No 6437 are captured amidst the throng of enthusiasts on 13 May 1961. *Colour-Rail*

Right:
No 8701 with the two auto-coaches is the centre of attraction during the tour of the Forest of Dean lines on 13 May 1961. *Colour-Rail*

Looking in superb condition as the evening sun catches
the gleaming paintwork, the restored 'Jones Goods' 4-6-0
No 103 takes water at Strathcarron whilst working an
Inverness-Kyle of Lochalsh timetabled passenger service.
The locomtive's condition is explained by the fact that this
was a running-in turn following its restoration.
Colour-Rail (P246)

1962

Isle of Wight Engines

Even after Grouping, when the Southern Railway inherited several rival companies, the railways of the Isle of Wight retained a remarkable degree of individuality which delighted enthusiasts. Besides lines developed by private companies, the 45-mile network taken over by the SR included the joint line of the London & South Western and London Brighton & South Coast railways between Ryde Pier Head and St John's Road.

From the moment of takeover, the SR realised the entire locomotive stock, consisting of a motley collection of veterans acquired by the individual companies, was hopelessly out of date. Two Class 02 0-4-4 tanks which William Adams built for LSWR suburban services and branch lines were quickly imported for testing. They were found to be ideal for the island's short-haul lines.

More than 20 were shipped from the mainland between 1923–49. The tanks, which always faced south because there was no turntable on the island, had their bunkers enlarged to lengthen the time they could spend off shed.

'W36' Carisbrooke, which arrived in 1949, was one of only two fitted for push-pull working. It ran on the 5½-mile Merstone–Ventnor West branch, but its reign there was short as the line closed in September 1952.

The 0-4-4 tanks did not quite establish a locomotive monopoly, for the island also had a small number of 'Terrier' 0-6-0 tanks, some of which had been working there before Grouping. And there were four Stroudley 'E1'

class 0-6-0 tanks for goods traffic. The island never saw tender engines.

Every locomotive was named after local places, with the notable omission of Parkhurst. The '02s' handled passenger trains restricted to six veteran coaches. They were crowded only during the summer holiday season because local passenger traffic was sparse. Freight traffic was almost exclusively coal being delivered via Medina Wharf near Cowes.

Locomotives were concentrated at Ryde shed after the closure of that at Newport in 1957. Holidaymakers crowded steam-hauled trains for the last time in 1966 for steam was withdrawn from the island at the end of the year. From the following March, the 'main line' between Ryde Pier Head and Shanklin was electrified with a third rail.

Below:
Class 02 No W33 *Bembridge* awaits departure from Ryde Pierhead on 29 August 1961. This locomotive was originally L&SWR No 218 and was built in August 1892. It was transferred to the Isle of Wight in May 1936, lasting 30 years on the island before withdrawal in December 1966, when all the remaining '02s' were taken out of service. *Colour-Rail*

Above right:
This delightful study sees '02' No W22 *Brading* appropriately running light engine at Brading on 8 June 1864. No W22, originally L&SWR No 215 built in June 1892, was amongst the earliest of the class to be transferred to the island (in June 1924). The locomotive was another casualty of the mass withdrawal of the '02s' at the end of 1966. *Colour-Rail*

Below right:
No W30 *Shorwell* is pictured at Wroxall on 12 August 1965 towards the end of its operational life; the locomotive was withdrawn the following month. No W30 was built as L&SWR No 219 in September 1962 and transferred to the Isle of Wight in April 1926. *Colour-Rail*

A Journey from Ryde to Ventnor

In 1953 J. Alan Rannie made a final journey over the Newport–Freshwater branch, 'the familiar and well-beloved line of my youth' as he recalled in *Trains Illustrated*. It closed in autumn of that year and Rannie lamented: 'It is good to know that though trains to Freshwater will, alas, run no more, the lines to Cowes, Ryde and Sandown will at least survive for a little longer.'

Today it is good to know that the forecast was rather pessimistic, although the island has suffered a host of railway economies. The 2¼-mile Brading–Bembridge branch closed on the same day as the Freshwater line, but the Cowes–Newport–Sandown passenger service survived until winter 1956 and that from Cowes via Newport to Ryde for another decade: until February 1966. Only weeks later, on 18 April, Ventnor was taken off the railway map, when the line was cut back to Shanklin.

And on 16 May — before the start of that year's holiday season — all freight services were withdrawn.

Since the Newport–Ryde closure, enthusiasts have reopened five miles of the route as the Isle of Wight Steam Railway. Their headquarters at Haven Street are always an interesting — and tidy — place to visit.

One of the strongest manifestations of its value to the tourist industry came in summer 1991 with the opening of an interchange with the Ryde–Shanklin line at Smallbrook Junction. Although used only when the preserved railway is operating, Smallbrook is the second station added to the main line in recent years. A station to serve the residential area of Lake between Sandown and Shanklin opened in May 1987.

Although sea breezes no longer snatch smoke out of the chimneys of Class 02 tanks, Ryde Pier is still a place where trains and ferries make frequent connections. In summer many passengers using the Portsmouth ferries travel to and from London, and current Isle of Wight passenger timetables detail services between Waterloo and Ventnor Bus Terminal (and also the island's main bus services).

Before Grouping, IOW travellers could catch London & South Western services from Waterloo or London Brighton & South Coast trains from Victoria or London Bridge.

In Edwardian days, the IOW Railway got businessmen who had spent the weekend on the island to the City before lunch by running a Mondays-only express from Ventnor. It departed at 7.25am and made booked stops at Shanklin and Sandown. Passengers for London, Portsmouth and Brighton could also signal it to stop at Wroxall and Brading Junction, where there was a connection off the Bembridge branch.

For years, holidaymakers arriving at Ryde Pier Head either caught a train from the four-platform terminal or, if they were not going further by rail, Drewry petrol railcars. They shuttled up and down the pier on tracks alongside those of the railway until 1969.

Pensioners wanting to recapture 'the good old days' now visit the IOW Steam Railway, hoping to be rewarded by the sight of 'W24' *Calbourne* heading a train of former island compartment stock. A minute or two spent watching the formation arriving at Wootton is sufficient to rekindle in memory the little trains that carried thousands of holidaymakers on the final stage of journeys to the seaside after they had crossed the Solent. The preserved line is the splendid reminder of a system quite different from all the other railways of Britain.

Reading

Allen, P. C. & McLeod, A. B., *Rails in the Isle of Wight*
Robbins, M., *The Isle of Wight Railways*

Ryde Pier Head–Ventnor

Distance:	12½ miles
Opened:	1862–1880
	20 March 1967 Ryde Pier Head–Shanklin electrified. Third rail.
Closed:	18 April 1966 Shanklin–Ventnor·

Left:
For most travellers to the Isle of Wight in the period, their first experience of the island was to be gained by landing, courtesy of the ferry, at Ryde Pier. Here, in August 1961, we see both ferry and train at Ryde Pier. The locomotive is 'O2' class 0-4-4T No 33 *Bembridge* and the paddle-steamer is, appropriately, *Ryde*.
The late J. P. Willett/Colour-Rail (BRS884)

Above:
South of Ryde, the lines to Cowes and Ventnor divided at Smallbrook Junction. Here 'O2' 0-4-4T No W29 *Alverstone* is held at the signals whilst heading south on 27 May 1961. The section from Ryde south to Shanklin, now electrified, remains open, whilst, through the efforts of the Isle of Wight Steam Railway steam trains now link Smallbrook Junction with Wootton, thus one again enabling this location to echo to the sound of an 'O2'.　　*Colour-Rail*

Below:
A panoramic view, taken from above the station at Ventnor shows No W27 *Merstone* running round its train on 8 June 1964. The section from Shanklin to Ventnor closed two years later, on 18 April 1966, although there has been pressure in recent years for it to be reopened.
The late J. P. Mullett/Colour-Rail

'Jones Goods'

A magnificent engine singing a magnificent song in a magnificent setting! Exaggerated, romanticised thinking? No! For here is a delightful sequence which took two years to film, as the commentary explains, of preserved Highland Railway No 103: the first 4-6-0 to run in Britain. It is shown on its old home territory of the 63½-mile Dingwall–Kyle of Lochalsh line completed (three years after the locomotive) in 1897. The route is sometimes called 'the other road to the Isles' to distinguish it from the old North British Glasgow–Fort William–Mallaig route: the West Highland Line.

As No 103 climbs stiff gradients its crisp bark echoes around the Highlands. This is an outstandingly nostalgic piece of actuality, perhaps the best reproduced on all the video tapes.

It was the first of a class of 15 locomotives built for the Highland Railway by Sharp Stewart and Company in 1894. Besides being the first 4-6-0s, they were also the most powerful main line engines in Britain. The title 'Jones Goods' by which the class is remembered, is slightly misleading. As *The Historic Locomotive Pocketbook* of H. C. Casserley explains: 'Although intended primarily for freight work they have also done much passenger duty in the height of the busy season and were of inestimable value to the Highland under its difficult operational conditions.'

It is perhaps difficult today to realise the impact made by the class. H. A. Vallance, a respected historian of the Highland Railway, states in his book of that title: 'The design was a radical departure from existing practice, and every credit is due to Jones for the bold way in which he broke with long established tradition by introducing an entirely new wheel arrangement.' Among small alterations made to some of the class, including No 103, was the fitting of a louvred chimney, an innovation which the HR introduced to a number of locomotive types, to lift the flow of smoke on long stretches of downhill running.

The 'Jones Goods' class was withdrawn by the LMS over the lengthy period of more than a decade between 1929 and 1940. No 103 was a comparatively early casualty, being taken out of service in 1934 and stored at St Rollox.

A quarter of a century later, it was restored to working order for the Scottish Industries Exhibition at which other preserved Scottish locomotives are seen on the 1959 tape.

There was a sense of historical importance about the train the Scottish Region selected for No 103 to haul. It was the early morning departure from the Kyle of Lochalsh which was then one of the last mixed passenger and goods trains running in Britain.

There was no suggestion in *Bradshaw's* timetables that it was mixed, though it was shown as terminating at Dingwall, with a through coach for Inverness. It was booked to take 3hr 20min to Dingwall, more than 30min more than the two later services of the day. Both continued to Inverness, nearly 19 miles south of Dingwall.

Left:
Heading eastwards, towards Dingwall, at Achnasheen on 20 May 1960, this view from the footplate of No 103 illustrates the superb scenery through which the Kyle of Lochalsh route travels. *Eric Russell/Colour Rail*

Above right:
Pictured on arrival at Dingwall on 20 May 1960, No 103 is naturally the centre of attractions. The Highland Railway first reached Dingwall in 1862, with the line being extended north to Invergordon the following year; the line to Strome Ferry opened in 1872. *Eric Russell/Colour-Rail*

Right:
Looking superb in the sunlight, No 103 heads eastbound along the shore of Loch Carron at Strome Ferry. In the background the 1,296ft high peak of Bad a' Chreamha provides a suitably dramatic background. Between 1872, when the line from Dingwall was opened, and 1897, when the line to Kyle of Lochalsh was completed, Strome Ferry was the line's terminus. *John Adams/Colour-Rail*

Kirtley Johnson & Co

Preservation of historical relics was important to many companies long before a national railway museum was ever seriously envisaged.

The opening of Britain's first railway museum at York in the 1920s was a marvellous piece of public relations. The success of the project (see 1960 tape) was in contrast to the efforts of the LNWR which never managed to justify a claim, which it made from Edwardian days in its typical boastful fashion, that it was 'arranging' the first railway museum in the British Empire at Euston. But the LNWR does deserve credit for preserving a number of locomotives and other relics which it kept at Crewe.

These are now part of the National Collection as are a group of ex-Midland Railway locomotives which were paraded in summer 1962. Three were 'pure' Midland Railway, the fourth, the green-liveried 4-4-2 tank *Thundersley,* was built for the London Tilbury & Southend Railway, which the Midland absorbed in 1912.

In keeping with Midland tradition, the parade went to the company's official photographic location at Wirksworth, at the end of an 8½-mile single branch from Duffield.

The locomotives were towed from Derby by the best known of the four: the Midland 'Compound' No 1000, a Johnson design of 1902. The MR only built 45 but after Grouping the LMS thought so highly of them that it constructed nearly 200 more.

The 'Compound' was the biggest of the group, but the most elegant was an earlier Johnson design: the 4-2-2 'Spinner'. Many think they were the loveliest engines ever built.

As the programme was essentially for children — 'young viewers' as they would be known today — they were encouraged to take part and at Wirksworth they did! They added almost a carnival spirit to the occasion — but how much did they remember of it? Does the sight of the locomotives preserved at York and elsewhere stir memories?

The Wirksworth branch has its own claim in history for it was among the last closed to passengers before Nationalisation. The LMS withdrew twice-daily stopping trains to and from Derby in summer 1947.

Reading
Gough, J., *The Midland Railway: A Chronology*, Published by Railway & Canal Historical Society

Duffield–Wirksworth	
Distance:	8½ miles
Owner:	Midland Railway
Opened:	1 October 1867
Closed:	16 June 1947 for Passengers
	1 April 1968 for Regular Goods traffic

Right:
Oldest of the quartet of locomotives recorded on the Wirksworth branch was 2-4-0 No 158A. Built originally to a design of Kirtley at Derby Works in October 1866 and rebuilt 15 years later, the locomotive became No 158A in 1896. It was rebuilt again the following year and became No 2 in 1907. Renumbered 20002 in 1934, it was withdrawn for preservation in July 1947. It is currently on display at the Midland Railway Centre. *John Adams/Colour-Rail*

Centre right:
One of a number of 'Singles' built for the Midland Railway towards the end of the 19th century, No 118 was built at Derby to a design of Johnson, who held sway from 1873 until 1903, in 1897. The locomotive was renumbered as 673 in 1907 and rebuilt two years later. Withdrawal and preservation came in April 1928, as the last of the type to remain in service. *John Adams/Colour-Rail*

Below:
No 1000 was the first of Deeley's Compound 4-4-0s and was built in October 1905. The first Compound 4-4-0s had been built for the Midland to the design of Johnson, but Deeley modified the design so that the locomotives started off in simple mode before switching to compound action once on the move. The locomotive was renumbered 1005 in 1907 (and hence became No 41005 on Nationalisation) and was fitted with a superheated boiler in 1923. It was withdrawn (for preservation) in 1951. *John Adams/Colour-Rail*

Left:
Predating the Midland Railway's takeover of the London, Tilbury & Southend Railway in 1911, this Whitelegg-designed 4-4-2T was built by Robert Stephenson & Co. Numbered 80 by the LT&S, it became MR No 2177 in 1912. It was withdrawn in 1956 as BR No 41966 and can now be seen at the Bressingham Museum. *John Adams/Colour-Rail*

The Bluebell Line

With the historic industrial Middleton Railway at Leeds, the Bluebell Railway was among the first standard gauge lines to be taken over and given fresh lives by enthusiasts.

The inspiration for the Bluebell project was that of three students who lifted their eyes to the mountains of North Wales. They felt what narrow gauge companies had achieved in and around Snowdonia could be repeated amid the quiet countryside of Southern England.

In winter 1959, the climate seemed ripe for a standard gauge project based on the line between Culver Junction just over 3 miles north of Lewes and East Grinstead, which BR had closed for a second time after a protracted and classic legal battle.

The birth of the project dated from the formation of the Bluebell Railway Preservation Society in June 1959 when, after the students had been joined by others, the Southern Region agreed to sell some 5 miles of the line between Sheffield Park and Horsted Keynes.

The key to the success was emphasised by R. C. Riley who wrote in the *Railway Magazine* in April 1962: 'Shrewd publicity at this stage — and indeed ever since — kept the Bluebell line in the public eye.'

Visits in 1961 and 1962 were at a time when the movement was facing many problems, partly because BR steam was still running everywhere and preserved steam railways did not have the novelty value or tourist appeal.

But infant preservation companies quickly recognised the need to establish their individual identities — something they are still having to do in an age when many lines are competing for patronage.

The Bluebell suffered an early setback when it was left in isolation after BR closed the electrified branch between Horsted Keynes and the Brighton main line at Haywards Heath in autumn 1963. There was the compensation of gaining access and full control of Horsted Keynes station. But severing the lifeline, over which enthusiast specials had been run through from London, has meant that the Bluebell will be unconnected until the extension to East Grinstead is completed. Meanwhile, current passenger timetables show a bus link.

While the Bluebell may have been without a main-line connection for many years longer than other preserved lines, it has remained one of Britain's best-advertised restored lines.

Culver Junction-East Grinstead

Distance:	17¼ miles
Owner:	London Brighton & South Coast Railway
Opened:	1 August 1882
Closed:	13 June 1955: Lewes–East Grinstead (21 miles) for Passengers, official date
Reopened:	7 August 1956
Closed:	17 March 1958 (BR)
Reopened:	7 August 1960 Sheffield Park–Horsted Keynes (4¾ miles) formally reopened by Bluebell Railway Preservation Society. Later extended Horsted Keynes–Kingscote (5 miles). Extension to East Grinstead (2 miles) under construction.

Horsted Keynes–Copyhold Junction–Haywards Heath

Distance:	4¾ miles
Owner:	London Brighton & South Coast Railway
Opened:	3 September 1883. Electrified by Southern Railway 7 July 1935
Closed:	26 October 1963 Passenger service withdrawn

Below:
The diminutive ex-London, Brighton & South Coast Railway 'Terrier' class 0-6-0Ts were to survive in service for many years. The first of the class were built in 1872 and the last were withdrawn in 1963; no less then eight are preserved. No 55 *Stepney* (formerly BR No 32655) is seen at Sheffield Park in July 1962. *Colour-Rail*

Above:
One of the 'foreign' locomotives to find a safe haven on the preserved Bluebell Railway at this time was ex-Great Northern Railway 0-6-0T No 1247, which is seen at Sheffield Park on 1 April 1962. Designed by Henry Ivatt, the 'J52' class was introduced in 1897. No 1247 was withdrawn (as BR No 68846) in 1959 and was bought for preservation by Capt Bill Smith, thus becoming the first standard gauge steam locomotive to be privately preserved. *Colour-Rail*

Below:
The only surviving Adams-designed Class 0415 Radial tank, No 488, had an eventful career before being preserved on the Bluebell Railway. Built in 1885 as London & South Western Railway No 488, it passed to the independent East Kent Railway as the latter's No 5 before being acquired by the Southern Railway (as No 3488) in 1946 for use on the Lyme Regis branch. Withdrawn by BR as No 30583 in 1961, the locomotive is seen here at Horsted Keynes on 1 April 1962. *Colour-Rail*

The 'Cambrian Coast Express'

The intense fascination of the railways of Wales is encapsulated in a scene at Machynlleth as a departing portion of the 'Cambrian Coast Express' runs past a sheep and its lamb walking between the platforms.

It was the sort of incident which gave the 'CCE' the image of a titled train which changed its character as it distanced itself from London.

The 'Cambrian Coast Express' was introduced by the GWR in 1927 and up to its demise with the end of steam timings never altered significantly. This was due partly to the number of places at which it stopped. It was integrated into Paddington–Birmingham (Snow Hill) services via Bicester and Banbury which, until 1966, was still a junction for the Great Central main line to South Yorkshire.

At Shrewsbury, the 'CCE' shed an English skin and acquired a Welsh one. Locomotives were changed, the restaurant car taken off and, in the early 1960s, replaced by an automatic buffet installed in one of the coaches.

Film of the 'CCE' calling at Moat Lane Junction is historic for at the end of 1962 this attractive 'Crewe in the country' closed with the Mid-Wales line. Its infrequent weekday trains called at the host of attractive towns on its faded nameboard: Llanidloes, Rhayader, Builth Wells and Brecon.

The three-storey station building which dominated a lonely stretch of the Severn Valley had a refreshment room, often busy because of commercial travellers and tourists, who for years sat complaining about having to make lengthy connections.

Any railway enthusiasts among them would have had time to visit the small Cambrian Railways shed which lay just off the Coast line and at right angles to the Brecon route. Allocated locomotives and visitors were sometimes veterans, perhaps the last examples of classes being scrapped. It was said that a couple of passengers on the last train to Brecon — an SLS special — got left behind at Moat Lane because of mistiming a dash to see what was on shed.

Moat Lane was a station where ex-GWR locomotives predominated on trains using the Cambrian Coast platform, while that for Brecon saw smaller locomotives and, in later years, far more BR standard types.

Beyond Machynlleth, where the 'CCE' split into Aberystwyth and Pwllheli portions, the express became almost a local train in nature and Western Region timetables demanded the attentive reading of passengers.

Beyond Machynlleth, the 'CCE' was booked to stop only at Borth, one of the five intermediate stations, but passengers who had travelled from beyond Shrewsbury could alight at neighbouring Llandre on notice being given to the guard at the previous *stopping* station.

The use of italics suggests there had been confusion in the past as to when intending passengers talked to the guard.

I came to admire the hardiness of Welsh locomotivemen when I made a return footplate trip to Aberystwyth on a bitter January day in 1964. I felt snug in the cab of a standard Class 4 2-6-4 tank, but terribly exposed to the elements riding the almost open footplate of No 7800 *Torquay Manor* on the early afternoon express to Shrewsbury.

Fortunately it was only a bitter gale-force wind — and not torrential rain — that swept in from behind as we pounded Talerddig bank with four coaches and a van, a load comfortably within the limits of a 'Manor' class 4-6-0.

The storm sheet remained furled under the cab roof. It would have been of little use.

Reading
Christiansen, R., and Miller, R. W., *The Cambrian Railways, Volume II: 1889–1968*
Green, G. C., *Cambrian Railways Albums 1 and 2*
Johnson, P., *The Cambrian Lines*

Right:
Heading the down 'Cambrian Coast Express'
'Manor' class No 7811 *Dunley Manor* makes a
fine sight as it passes Moat Lane on 31 July 1959.
Colour-Rail

Below:
Pictured at Machynlleth on 24 May 1962 in the
early summer sunlight, 'Manor' class No 7823
Hook Norton Manor drifts towards the
cameraman with the 'Cambrian Coast Express'.
The late Malcolm Thompson/Colour-Rail

Left:
Seen under the overall roof at Shrewsbury station
prior to its removal, 'Manor' class 4-6-0 No 7803
Barcote Manor awaits departure with the
'Cambrian Coast Express' in May 1961. The
Western Region started a rebuilding programme
at Shrewsbury station during 1961, and the
overall roof gradually succumbed between then
and 1964. *C. J. B. Sanderson/Colour-Rail*

Right:
Journey's end. 'Manor' class 4-6-0 No 7818
Granville Manor approaches Aberystwyth with
the down 'Cambrian Coast Express'.
Keith Bannister/Colour-Rail

Western Region Engines

More than three decades after the *Railway Roundabout* visit to Swindon, the video is a reminder of the interest and excitement spotters found during the years of BR modernisation.

Several visits were made to the works when steam was giving way to diesel power yet both forms of traction were working alongside each other during a fascinating period of transition.

No 7023 *Penrice Castle* was one of the last of the class to be built at Swindon, a town with which the 'Castles' had another close association through hauling the 'Cheltenham Flyer' — the world's fastest train in the early 1930s. Swindon was the junction from which it began its high-speed dash to Paddington. Between Cheltenham Spa and Swindon timings were modest because of a number of booked stops and heavy, twisting Cotswold gradients.

The GWR heavily publicised the 'Cheltenham Flyer', but in *Bradshaw's* it was always the 'Cheltenham Spa Express Tea Car Train'.

It still held its famous title after the birth of the GWR's own diesel age. Evidence is to be found in the Cardiff, Newport, Gloucester, Cheltenham Spa and London services table of winter 1936. A footnote detailed another service operated by a 'streamlined Rail Car, one class only (limited accommodation)'.

More than 170 'Castles' were built in programmes which lasted beyond Nationalisation. Some of their workings were eventually taken over by 'Britannia' class Pacifics with a profile which looked more modern than the stately outline of the 'Castles'. The 'Britannias' were the first of twelve standard designs which BR planned to build in large numbers to replace older types inherited from the Big Four post-Grouping companies. Crewe built 55 from 1951 and one of those allocated to the Western Region was No 70025 *Western Star*, a reminder of the GWR 'Star' class 4-6-0s from which the 'Castles' were developed.

As the diesel age dawned, the Western Region persuaded the British Transport Commission to let it test the diesel hydraulic system when new locomotives were ordered and the 'Warship' and 'Western' classes gradually took over named and other expresses from 'Castles' and 'Britannias'.

Just after World War 1, Swindon built a small class of what were officially called 'Express Mixed and Perishable Goods Traffic Engines'. Numbered 4700–4708, they were never as successful as Churchward's 2-8-0 mineral class of 1903: the first of its type in Britain.

A reminder of the importance and growth of the Great Western's London suburban services is the presence at Swindon of a '61xx' class 2-6-2 tank: one of the 'Large Prairies' as the class was known. C. B. Collett introduced the class in the early 1930s to meet the growing traffic demands for the services on lines into Paddington from areas east of Maidenhead and High Wycombe.

The commentator refers to Swindon as the spiritual home of GWR enthusiasts. In late Victorian times, the works were open to visitors on Wednesday afternoons. Was many a boy's love of railways born when father took son on a works visit and introduced him to 'God's Wonderful Railway'?

Reading

Chapman, W. G., *GWR Engines, Names, Numbers, Types, Classes etc*

Cooper, B. K., *BR Motive Power Since 1948*

Peacock, T. B., *Great Western London Suburban Services*

Below:
'Castle' class 4-6-0 No 7023 *Penrice Castle* is seen in ex-works condition outside Swindon. This locomotive was built in June 1949. This photograph was taken after May 1958, as No 7023 had a double chimney fitted that month. No 7023 was to remain in service until February 1965 and was amongst the last 'Castle' class locomotives to remain in service.
A. Sainty Collection/Colour-Rail

Above:
Pictured on the turntable at Swindon in 1961, No 70025 *Western Star* was one of the 'Britannia' class Pacifics allocated to the Western Region from new. Delivered to Cardiff Canton — the first of a batch of five to be based there — in September 1952, No 70025 was, like the remainder of the class, ultimately to end its life on the London Midland Region, being withdrawn from Carlisle Kingmoor in December 1967.
John Adams/Colour-Rail

Below:
'Warship' class diesel-hydraulic No D802 is seen at Swindon in August 1963. Named *Formidable,* No 802 was one of only three of the 'Warships' — along with Nos D800 and D801 — that were not permitted to operated in multiple. It was these three locomotives that were the first of the B+B 'Warships' to be withdrawn, in 1968, No D802 succumbing in the October of that year. The locomotive was cut up, exactly two years later (in October 1970), at Swindon Works. *Colour-Rail*

Seaton Junction

The last study made by the programme team was of the Waterloo–Exeter West of England main line which by 1962 was the last one in Britain being worked purely by steam. And what a feast the cameras filmed on a summer's day at Seaton Junction, 148 miles from Waterloo, lying within sight of Devon's green and rolling hills.

Expresses hauled by a host of Southern Region locomotives coming to the end of top-link lives rushed non-stop through the two middle roads, or halted at the long platforms to detach and attach summer-Saturday only through-coaches on the branch to the little resort of Seaton. Frequent two-coach push-pull services in charge of 'M7' class 0-4-4 tanks were allowed 12min for 4½ mile journeys with stops at Colyton and Colyford.

A West of England departure from Waterloo at about 11am was named the 'Atlantic Coast Express' by the Southern Railway in 1926 when it became famous as the most multi-portioned express running in Britain, detaching coaches between Salisbury and Ilfracombe. Seaton was the first of a number of small resorts to have its own through-service. A coach detached at Salisbury was attached to a following service which called at stations to Seaton Junction and then reversed down the branch.

The Southern Railway published a 'from the carriage window' guide for the 'ACE' by the well known travel writer S. P. B. Mais, and another called *Let's Get Out Here* detailing 26 walks from places on the route. It demanded some athleticism by holidaymakers for in the 1937 edition, Mais noted that the 'ACE' reached Seaton at 3 o'clock. That meant there was plenty of time for 'a pleasant afternoon walk to find one's sea legs'. The suggested walk was one of only 'about four or five miles'.

In autumn 1961, the Southern Region speeded up the 'ACE' on the day that the Western Region decelerated its diesel-hauled services including the 'Cornish Riviera Express'. David St. J. Thomas said in his *Regional History of Railways of the West Country* that steam's swan-song on the Waterloo–Exeter line had earned considerable patronage at the expense of the Western line.

But such enterprise was soon to end for in March 1966 Seaton Junction was among many intermediate stations closed between Salisbury and Exeter. It was an economy overshadowed by the entire closure of the Somerset & Dorset line, which took place on the same day.

Tourists in their thousands have since travelled over the Seaton branch trackbed which for three miles north from the resort carries the 2ft 9in gauge Seaton & District Electric Tramway.

Reading
Allen, C. J., *Titled Trains of Great Britain*
Whitehouse, P., & Thomas, D. St. J., *The Great Days of the Southern Railway*

Seaton Junction–Seaton	
Owner:	London & South Western Railway
Opened:	16 March 1868
Closed:	7 March 1966

Below:
Class M7 No 30045 is seen on 19 April 1960, in the rolling Devon countryside near Seaton Junction. Passenger services over the Seaton branch were withdrawn on 7 March 1966, although that was not quite the end of the story as part of the trackbed is now utilised for the very successful Seaton Tramway. *Colour-Rail*

Above right:
Class M7 0-4-4T No 30125 departs from Seaton Junction with a push-pull set in 1960. No 30125 was constructed as LSWR No 125 in November 1911; it was withdrawn from Exmouth Junction shed in December 1962. *J. G. Dewing/Colour-Rail (BRS11)*

Below right:
No 30045 is seen again at Seaton in 1960. Like No 30125, No 30045 was resident at Exmouth Junction prior to withdrawal in December 1962, although this particular locomotive was slightly older, being constructed in May 1905. *Colour-Rail*

Can You Guess?

The series ended on a note of mystery by recalling a 'Can You Guess?' location competition was featured in each programme.

In the 1962 video, viewers are left to identify four locations — without any answers being given. But the type of locomotives shown at each place should provide good clues to each answer.

While the *Railway Roundabout* programmes were compiled to appeal to young viewers and screened around tea-time, John Adams and Pat Whitehouse made no secret of their hopes that they would appeal to Dad as well.

They wrote a companion book with the same title as the programmes hoping that it would be 'some small compensation for the large number of "older children" who cannot get home from work in time to see them'.

That was in an age when there were no home video recorders. But there was still plenty of steam although that was under threat. This was made clear from one of the book's illustrations. It heralded a 'Midland Pullman' diesel set as the 'Train of the Future'.

Below:
One of the four mystery locations featured in the 'Can you Guess' section at the end of the 1962 film was a well-known incline to the southwest of Birmingham. Here '4F' 0-6-0 No 43853 passes Bromsgrove station with a freight on 20 April 1957. *R. C. Riley*

Front cover: No 7031 *Cromwell's Castle* leaves Paddington with the 4.45pm to Wolverhampton in June 1962.
P. W. Gray/Colour-Rail (BRW 411)

Back cover, top: The preserved ex-Caledonian Single No 123 was recorded well away from its home teritory when, on 15 September 1963, this view at Norwood Junction was taken. *R. C. Riley*

Back cover, bottom: The Hayling Island branch, with its diminutive ex-LBSCR 'Terrier' 0-6-0Ts, was a firm favourite with enthusiasts before steam working ceased and the line closed. Here No 32662 is portrayed near Havant on 2 November 1963. By this date both the line and the locomotive were in their last days of operation; the branch was due to close completely two days later. *R. C. Riley*